The very best
MEMORIES
from
MANCHESTER

CONTENTS

INTRODUCTION

Without too much of a doubt, Manchester is the city that is the capital of the North of England. Liverpuddlians will argue their case, as will those from Leeds or even Newcastle, but we know where the truth lies. This fine city of ours has long been the epicentre of cultural development and industrial growth. Its sons and daughters have been at the forefront of revolution in everything from technology and politics to music and literature. Physicist and Nobel prize winner JJ Thompson, suffragette Emmeline Pankhurst, prime minister David Lloyd George, the Gallagher brothers of Oasis fame and author Anthony Burgess are just a handful of famous names who first saw the light of day here.

However, 'Memories from Manchester' does not concentrate on the achievements of the high and mighty. It focuses more on the everyday lives of people who helped make the old 'cottonopolis' what it was and shape the modern city into what it has become. Turning the pages and looking at the glorious photographs on them, the reader will be able to rejoin grandpa as he walks through the streets of Moss Side on his way to take his place on the terraces at the Kippax Stand and cheer another thrilling save by Bert Trautmann. On another occasion, there is a chance to go back to Piccadilly Gardens when they were full of shopgirls from Paulden's department store taking a well earned break at lunchtime. The air was full of chatter about what it had been like in days gone by to listen to the clatter of the looms as they turned out yard after yard of material in the mills. This was the trade that provided so many of the population with their livelihood and so many of the owners with their wealth. Although associated with the textile industry for several centuries, it was not until Arkwright constructed the first purpose built cotton mill in 1780 that the industrial revolution began in Manchester and changed its nature forever.

In this book there is ample evidence of how the city evolved during the last century. On one page there are trams and on another it is multi storey car parks and pedestrianised areas. Large malls now dominate where shops with their own individuality once stood. Fashions and styles are so different when comparing one era with another. The floor length dresses of the Edwardians gave way to the short flapper skirts of the roaring 20s. After the last war, the hemline fell, only to rise dramatically in the swinging 60s. Men favoured suits and headwear throughout the first two thirds of the 20th century, before they were abandoned for more casual styles. Attitudes and values also changed, though we can only guess at these from the photographs in 'Memories from Manchester'.

Still, you can always prepare for the wonderfully nostalgic trip down this local memory lane by putting a Hollies 45 rpm record on the Dansette. 'Just one look' would be a good choice. Then, pour yourself a glass of Vimto and you are ready for all these delights from yesteryear.

First published in Great Britain by True North Books Limited
England HX3 6AE
01422 344344

ISBN 978-1906649265

Text, design and origination by True North Books Limited
Printed and bound by The Charlesworth Group

EVENTS & OCCASIONS

police force came into being after the setting up of a Watch Committee in 1839 and an office was established on Cross Street. Manchester City Police did not take control at Southmill Street until 1937 when special laboratories for forensics, fingerprints and photography were opened. In the 1930s each horse cost £75 and by the mid 1950s there were only 19 such animals on police duty. Most of these were used in assisting officers on traffic duty. Stables and a training centre were opened at Hough End in 1976 and by 1980 there were 40 horses at the disposal of the mounted police, increasingly being used in crowd control, especially outside football grounds.

Below: There is a touch of majesty about the sight of a detachment of mounted police riding imperiously along the road. The upright posture of both horse and rider indicates a touch of superiority in the constable and his steed. On the corner of Cobourg Street and Whitworth Street the 1936 law enforcement team was not just employed for show because there had been occasions when it was called into action. Oswald Mosley's British Union of Fascists were notorious trouble makers, stirring up feelings at rallies when tempers often got the better of normally placid souls who allowed themselves to be stirred by the rhetoric of the orator. Disaffected members of the ranks of the unemployed felt the weight of the force on horseback as their meetings were cleared when they became unruly. Manchester's

Top right: Life was tough in the 1930s for the working classes during the depression years when the country's economy struggled to make headway. Unemployment was high and wages were cut, leading to strikes, marches and a 'them and us' attitude existing between the haves and have nots. The cares of the world are etched in the face of the woman in the foreground. What a hard life she must have had. Born in the Victorian era she had been brought up in overcrowded housing that lacked proper sanitation, electricity or even the most basic living standards that we now take for granted. She had waved her husband off as he marched away to war in 1914, welcomed him back a disillusioned man after his experiences in the trenches and then tried to rebuild for a future 'fit for

heroes' as the government had glibly promised. Despite all the knock backs she could still be proud to be British and a loyal supporter of the monarchy. On Malcolm Street, Clayton she and her neighbours had prepared the tables for a street party in honour of the silver jubilee celebrations for King George V. On 6 May 1935 the nation got together in the biggest demonstration of unity since Armistice Day in 1918, but once the parties were over and the decks cleared it was back to life on a shoestring.

Right: The 1930s were a struggle for ordinary folk as wages were cut, living conditions failed to improve and unemployment rose to 3,000,000. There were pitched street battles between the police and disaffected workers and hunger marches on the capital included a Lancashire contingent in 1932. Aldous Huxley published 'Brave New World', but little could be seen of it at that time. The jobless were still marching in 1936 when men from Jarrow, a northeast town with 68 per cent of its workforce out of a job, hit the road on a five week journey. It came as no surprise to see the rise in popularity of such minor, but disruptive, political groups as the British Union of Fascists and the National Workers' Movement. The leaders of the day used a mixture of bully boy tactics and softly softly approaches to hold things in check. The Royal Family played its part by being seen to take an interest in the lives of

its subjects, though from the look on the faces of these Mancunians this visit was hardly inspirational. The Prince of Wales toured Britain in the early 1930s, often concentrating on workingmen's clubs, and enlisted more than 200,000 men and women in occupational schemes. During these years his popularity rose to a level achieved by his grandfather when he held the same title. However, his star waned in 1936 when, as King Edward VIII, news of his desire to wed the twice divorced American socialite, Wallis Simpson, became public. He abdicated five months before his scheduled coronation.

Right, below and top right: The war was over, and the citizens of Manchester were tired of bombs, gas masks, the blackout and all the other privations of wartime Britain. Out came the flags and the bunting and the photograph of good old 'Winnie', as Winston Churchill was affectionately known. Dust was blown off the accordion, and this entire community went wild with joy when the news that everybody was waiting for was announced. It was good to be alive, and along with the rest of Britain they found the energy to let their hair down and organise a knees-up. There was to be no immediate let up in the food rationing that Britain had grown used to during the war, however. In fact a year later in 1946 bread went on ration, though the first bananas that had been seen since before the war

arrived from the West Indies. Children born during the war had never seen a banana before, and had no idea that they had to peel off the skin before they could eat them.

For a good while to come saccharin tablets still went into tea cups in place of sugar, and (reputedly) whale oil margarine was still spread on the nation's bread.

Below right: When peace was declared in 1945 the blackout curtains could come down and there was an end to those wardens and their bellowing 'Turn that light out'. Beacons blazed on hilltops across the country and in city centres there were giant firework displays with rockets fizzing and sparking as they rushed up into the night sky. Even public transport was used as way of expressing the nation's joy and brightly illuminated victory trams, looking like something purloined from the Blackpool illuminations, trundled along their tracks. Only those who lived through the dark and dismal wartime days can appreciate what it felt like to have lights gleaming in the evening once more.

For nearly six years the only illumination had been provided by the bursting of shells, tracer bullets ripping through the air and the glow created by burning houses and factories after an air raid. Light had literally come back into the world and it was the herald of a bright future, or so the country hoped. In the general election that July the electorate turned to a new breed of politicians to take it forward into the second half of the century. Labour swept into power with a massive majority of 180 over the Tories. Prime Minister Attlee promised, 'We can deliver the goods.' In 1951 the public decided they hadn't and turned back to Churchill once more.

Left: Best foot forward, ma'am, and what a pretty foot it was as well in 1950. Sadly, it was to be a part of Princess Margaret's anatomy that was to cause her great distress in the final years leading up to her death in February 2002. She scalded herself badly and, although not the cause of her death, added to her decline from the vibrant and radiant woman she had once been. This visit to Manchester was one of many ceremonial duties she began to take on as a major royal figure after the war. Her work was to become even more important and her official life much busier once her sister had acceded to the throne in 1952. Born on 21 August 1930 Princess Margaret Rose was but a slip of a young woman when she visited Manchester, yet it is obvious from the admiring glances of the men in the crowd that here was a beauty who would continue to turn heads. She was something of a rebellious and forthright person, as second children often are, and soon made her way into the gossip columns of national newspapers with her

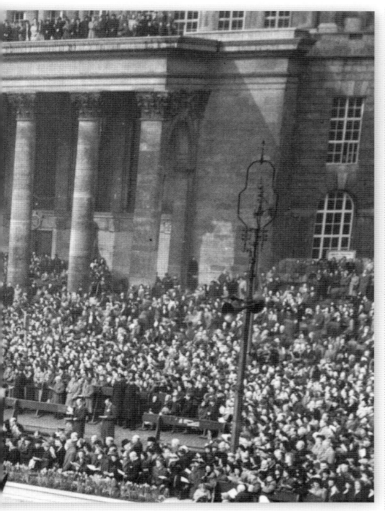

and variety theatres were packed out once again and fairgrounds and circuses had guaranteed support. Mancunians came to St Peter's Square to honour their royal guest, but mainly to remember the dead. The scene outside Central Library is a little different now since the Metrolink trams began to run past, but the Midland to the left remains. Located in the heart of the city, the Midland has witnessed some of the most notable meetings of the last century. Notably that of Charles Stewart Rolls and Fredrick Henry Royce, leading to the creation of Rolls Royce Ltd

comments and social whirl. It was her affair with Group Captain Peter Townsend that was to move her onto the front pages in 1955 when it seemed certain that she was going to announce marriage to her father's former equerry. He was a divorced man and the establishment feared ructions that might rival the 1936 abdication crisis. Princess Margaret eventually gave in to the pressure and severed connections with Townsend, but she never looked as happy again.

Above: After the war there was much rebuilding to be undertaken as we repaired huge tracts of land laid waste by the ravages of the bombing blitzes of the early 1940s. We also had to rebuild ourselves as a people and we took every opportunity that we could to turn out in large numbers to show solidarity. A service held at the Cenotaph was enough of a reason to come along and pay corporate respects, but this one had the added incentive of being attended by Queen Elizabeth, the mother of our present monarch. In 1949 the country was trying its best to get back to normal. Sporting venues were filled to bursting by huge crowds denied the pleasure of watching top-notch soccer, cricket and speedway for so many years. Cinemas

Top: Quite what the two pianos on the stage were doing during a religious rally at Belle Vue's King's Hall in 1950 is not clear. Perhaps Rawitz and Landauer, a pair of classical musicians who were forever appearing as guests to try and add a touch of the highbrow to variety shows in the 1950s, were due to perform later the following evening. It takes all sorts and King's Hall had more than its share of mixed events and people headlining its functions. There were political rallies, festivals, conferences, variety acts, wrestling and bingo bonanzas. They all added spice to the life of the well patronised building, but the most fondly remembered occasions have to be reserved for the times when the circus performers went through their routines. Glamorous girls standing on the backs of horses galloping around the ring, lion tamers going through their death defying routines, acrobats, tightrope walkers and the trapeze artists were part of a magical show. Then there were the true speciality acts, such as Captain Harry Schmidt and Evelyn with their sealions clapping their flippers and playing tunes on horns that they honked with their snouts. How the children loved to laugh at the antics of Jacko Fossett as he clowned about for three decades until the circus closed down in 1981.

Right: Garlands, streamers and the proud flags of St George waving over King Street in 1953 heralded the coronation of 2 June 1953. Elizabeth II had come to the throne on 6 February 1952, but the country had to wait nearly 16 months for the official period of mourning to end and preparations be made for the ceremonial coronation. It was an event that had a remarkable spin off in television sales. The goggle box was still in its infancy and few households possessed one, but the BBC had overcome narrow minded resistance from the establishment and had persuaded the powers that be to allow cameras into Westminster Abbey to screen the event. From that day on the importance of radio as the main source of news and entertainment in the home was to start to decline. Neighbours who had bought a little box with its flickering black and white screen suddenly discovered that they had a host of friends on their street as people crowded into their front rooms to listen to the rich, sonorous tones of Richard Dimbleby describing the events that unfolded before him. The decorations on King Street had twice been put to good use in 1945 when we celebrated VE and VJ Day, but after Coronation Day they could be put away for another 25 years until the Silver Jubilee came along.

Below: King Street is one of the most important thoroughfares of the city that connects Cross Street North to Deansgate. Once the centre of the north-west banking industry it is now predominantly designer fashion. Now pedestrianised, it is now recognised as a shoppers paradise and boasts top High Street brand names like Armani, Agent Provocateur, Monsoon, Ted Baker, DKNY and Vivienne Westwood. In 1953 cars could comfortably make their way along here without the restrictions that came into force in the latter decades of the 20th century. The Ford Popular and other cars were a reminder of Henry Ford's statement that customers could have any colour they wanted as long as it was black. Half a century ago we did not have the exotic shades and metallic hues available to the modern motorist. Somehow the drab colours seemed to suit the austere times, but at least there was a splash of colour in the Coronation decorations fluttering in the breeze. St George was well to the fore amongst the flowers and garlands that complemented the banners hung in celebration of that memorable day that gave the whole country a lift. Goodness how we needed it!

Above: Preparations for the Queen's coronation were just about complete at the end of May 1953. Flags fluttered in the breeze in what turned out to be several days of rather unseasonable weather. When the great day dawned the rain clouds gathered but the intermittent showers did not dampen the ardour of the crowds tucked in behind the crash barriers who turned out to witness the procession through Albert Square. Down in the capital a sea of people turned out to line the route to Westminster Abbey and witness the presence of representatives from the far corners of the British Commonwealth paying homage to Her Majesty. One of the most impressive figures was that cut by Queen Salote of Tonga, a huge and beaming figure who waved vigorously to the crowds as her open carriage rapidly filled with rainwater pouring down upon her. When Dr Fisher, the Archbishop of Canterbury, placed St Edward's Crown upon our new sovereign's head he must have said his own silent prayer of good luck for the 27 year old who was setting off on a royal voyage that the nation hoped would bring Britain into a new Elizabethan age. The monarch had inherited a country still suffering the economic effects of an expensive war and her subjects dearly wished that with her accession we would all be able to move forward into the better times that lay ahead.

Centre: At Kendal's, Santa Claus had a better class of Christmas present in his grotto than most other department stores, though it cost mum and dad a bit extra for the privilege. That probably did not mean too much because you needed a few bob to your name in 1953 to be able to do much more than browse through the various floors before settling for a cup of coffee. Even that was served at greater than Kardomah prices. Kendal Milne was largely reserved for the middle classes in those days, the sort of people who cried 'mansion!' when they filled a bingo card. The average man's weekly wage was about £10 and that of his wife just half of that. The clientele became more varied as greater spending power was more widely available in later years, but the store still retained a certain status. In recent years, however, it has lost some of its independent feel as other retail outlets have taken over some of the space behind its sweeping frontage. Kendal, Milne and Faulkner were partners in the middle of the 19th century, beginning in business when they bought a shopping bazaar from S & J Watts in 1836. The partnership originally concentrated on silks, but when Faulkner died in 1862 his name was dropped and in 1870 Kendal Milne opened on Deansgate. Lewis's was to be one of its main rivals, but at this stage of its trading history Kendal Milne concentrated on drapery and furniture, leaving Lewis's to develop its clothing sales.

Below: The Whit Walks were a tradition that brought even the greatest of cities to a standstill. Marching bands led the way and church groups unfurled their banners and the faithful proudly walked along behind. In Market Street in 1955 even office workers in the Exchange buildings put their pens to one side and looked down upon the delightful parade heading towards them. The pavement was covered by a seething mass of people who took great pleasure in the spectacle and proud mums joined in by walking with their little ones so beautifully dressed for the occasion. Garlands of flowers, little posies and pretty headdresses all added to the sense of pageantry. The girls held on to their streamers as some tried to perform a sort of maypole dance as they went along. It usually ended in confusion, but what did it matter? Everyone enjoyed the day and that was the main purpose of the walks. Traditionally, children all got new clothes and after they had finished their procession the youngsters went off to visit an old auntie or uncle they had not seen for ages, hopeful of a small addition to their piggy banks. 'Must be Whitsun, then', muttered one grumpy relative as he answered the door being pounded by an eager little tot. On returning home the new outfits were put away for use on future high days and holidays.

Right: In 1958 Jane Morgan sang about the day that the rains came down. Perhaps the composer had passed through Albert Square three years earlier and witnessed this scene. When Queen Elizabeth II made her 1955 visit to our city the greeting may have been warm but the day was decidedly horrid. But it did not dampen the spirits of the largely female crowd that turned out to welcome its royal guest. Long calf length coats, pacamacs, rainhoods and brollies were the fashion order of the day. It says much for both Mancunian loyalty to the crown and typical northern determination that so many braved the elements to cheer a young monarch, still in her 20s. There was a touch of glamour about the Queen, something we had not seen in her shy father. She was also a woman who needed our support, thrust into the forefront of public attention at such a tender age when George VI died in 1952. Queen Elizabeth attracted crowds like some modern pop star and, wherever she went, the streets would be lined with cheering wellwishers. Never mind that the pavements were glistening with rain and that the water just poured down the backs of our necks, we were British and we had come to show the rest of the nation, especially those southern softies, that a spot of inconvenience would not prevent us from showing the flag.

Below: During 1977 it appeared that the younger generation born in the late 1940s, many of them with young children of their own by then, had scant regard for the monarchy. Some of their attitudes towards the Royal Family rubbed off on their elders and it seemed as if the Queen's Silver Jubilee was going to be something of a damp squib. How odd that things changed so dramatically in the final few weeks leading up to the celebrations that marked the completion of 25 years of her reign. The official date of the anniversary was obviously that of her father's death and as it was hardly appropriate to hold parties to coincide with that, seven days in early June were designated as Silver Jubilee Week. From a slow start there was a sudden flurry of activity as the nation rediscovered patriotism. Bunting flew from lampposts and across roads, schools organised fancy dress competitions, memorial coins and mugs were dished out and people partied in the streets as old and young had a memorable knees up. Holywood Street, Moss Side had its tea party, tables and chairs were dragged out onto the pavement. and couples danced to Abba's 'Knowing me, Knowing you' and rounded off the session with loud choruses of 'Rule Britannia'.

Above: A Royal Variety Show at the Palace Theatre in 1959 saw Queen Elizabeth, the Queen Mother, gracing the occasion with her presence. That winning smile greeted the stars to whom she was presented just as it would for more than 40 years until her death at Easter 2002. Here was a woman as old as the 20th century, having been born on 4 August 1900 in Hertfordshire, though she spent much of her childhood at Glamis on Tayside. The Queen Mum, as she became affectionately known, was a highly respected and much loved royal. Here she was being introduced to one of the most glamorous stars of the 1950s. Liberace was a fine concert pianist who branched out into the world of variety, bringing to it a glitz that was years ahead of its time. With his candelabra atop of his piano and his outrageously sequinned costumes this American could command huge fees for his stage and television work. He won damages from the Daily Mirror's gossip columnist Cassandra in June 1959 when it was implied that he was a homosexual. The flamboyant Wladziu Valentino Liberace died on 4 February 1987. Other famous names in the line-up that year included, Marty Wilde, Anne Shelton, pianist Russ Conway, Jimmy Jewel, Arthur Askey, Benny Hill and the Tiller Girls.

Right: Even our parents grudgingly admitted that there was something likeable about the quartet of cheeky Liverpuddlians who took the mid 1960s by storm with their yeah, yeah, yeah and introduced the word Beatlemania into our language. Mum and dad might have winced at their mophead haircuts and some of the loud tunes they played, but they seemed like nice boys underneath. But, when it came to the Rolling Stones then that was a totally different matter. Much to their parents' disgust these young fans, seen in 1965 on Oxford Street, were ready to enter the Palace Theatre and scream their heads off in support of Mick, Brian, Keith, Bill and Charlie. The Stones were anathema to the older generation as they represented everything that was wrong with the youth of the day, in its opinion. They wore scruffy clothes, looked unkempt, wore their hair at a ridiculous length, played their music at an ear splitting level and were known to dabble in drugs. Teenagers loved them. In the theatre the Rolling Stones could have played any song they wished because the audience never heard a note as it was too busy screaming the house down.

Christmas was coming in 1958 and the band and choristers were out in force in Piccadilly Valley Gardens providing a lunchtime concert for shoppers and office workers. Santa and his reindeer, in front of a Christmas tree backdrop, took a short rest from their busy schedule to listen to 'We three kings' or 'Away in a manger'. Those were the days when children carried lanterns and came round to our houses singing their carols and we invited them in for a mince pie and gave them a tanner for entertaining us. They do not come any more as their parents will not let them onto the streets at night and anyone asking a youngster to step across the threshold would be thought to have ulterior motives. Modern society has consigned such youthful innocence to the waste bin. Half a century ago children thrilled to the sight of a nurse's uniform or Dinky car in their stockings with a magic colouring book as an added extra. Now they demand and get designer clothes and the latest electronic gizmos. When did you last see a kiddie playing imaginatively by using the furniture as a fort for his toy soldiers or as a hospital for her dolls? When was the last time that the Salvation Army band came up your street and stopped on the corner to play 'Once in Royal David's City'?

Left: At long last Matt Busby had achieved his dream and the European Cup could adorn the trophy cabinet at Old Trafford. A former Manchester City player, as United's new manager he had taken over a bomb wrecked ground and depleted team after the war. He took the first of his great sides to FA Cup triumph in 1948 and the League Championship in 1952, but then began to unravel the team as he developed the Busby Babes' policy of bringing in young talent. This wonderful set of young men won the title again in 1956 and were entered in the European Cup, a competition for champion clubs only. Despite objections from the dinosaurs in the Football Association, United swept all before them until they came up against the great Real Madrid, losing in the semi finals. Busby won the league title again in 1957 and his boys reached the European Cup semi final again, only to be cruelly struck down by the Munich air crash in 1958 that claimed the lives of eight players. During the 1960s another new side emerged, again reaching the European semi final in 1967 and going one better in 1968 when, at long last, that elusive trophy was lifted in a 4-1 defeat of Benfica. Busby and two survivors of the Munich disaster, Bobby Charlton and Bill Foulkes, shared a silent tear as the crowds cheered the arrival of the team for its civic reception at the Town Hall.

Above: In 2002 how could we have doubted the support the country would show for Queen Elizabeth II's Golden Jubilee? The scenes of over 1,000,000 flag waving subjects cheering the procession on its way to Buckingham Palace warmed the heart of every true Brit. That it heralded England's defeat of Argentina in the World Cup and Lennox Lewis flattening Mike Tyson made it something even more special. The same reservations had been held 25 years earlier when we prepared to acknowledge a quarter of a century of duty. Yet, when the time came the streets were filled with happy, smiling faces all enjoying the special occasion and the festivities that accompanied it. Moss Side held a carnival and buses and lorries were commandeered for the day and turned into gaily decorated floats. A week of celebrations began on 7 June 1977 when a giant bonfire was lit in Windsor Great Park. As the flames illuminated the evening sky 100 other bonfires were lit by Lord Lieutenants, Mayors and Bishops from Land's End to the Shetlands. In Manchester it seemed that every street had its own wildly successful party, though cynics could be heard to say that we would never again see their like.

ON THE HOME FRONT

Below: It is incorrect to label these men as Withington Home Guard because they were still Local Defence Volunteers (LDV) in the spring of 1940. The woman with her children provided the only spectators to this march past, but in the years to come thousands would turn out to acknowledge the role played by these volunteers and other members of the civil defence. At the end of the war the prime minister told the nation that the WVS, Red Cross, St John Ambulance, Land Army, ATS, Home Guard and the other various auxiliary groups formed the army that Hitler forgot. The men in this photograph were ready to stand firm if an invasion ever came and, in the meantime, lend a hand on other civil defence duties. The highly popular TV sitcom of the 1970s, 'Dad's Army', did these men little justice. Whilst it was very funny, it tended to belittle the work and dedication of these volunteers. It is true that in the LDV's early days there were instances of drills being carried out by men marching with broomsticks across their shoulders, but by the time they were renamed the Home Guard in July 1940 things had changed. Then this fine body of men, unarmed in this photograph, would be able to parade and practice with real weaponry, though, in truth, the range of equipment was still limited.

In the late 1930s we were slow to recognise that another major war was inevitable. Civil defence seemed to be a series of exercises for men playing at being soldiers and panicking unnecessarily. In 1937, when Fascist forces bombed the cultural and spiritual home of the Basques during the Spanish Civil War, it gave many of us an uneasy feeling. The destruction of Guernica was a mere foretaste of what was to come, but we were foolishly reassured by Prime Minister Chamberlain who returned from his meeting with Adolf Hitler in Munich in 1938 waving a piece of paper that promised 'peace in our time'. When the tanks rolled into Czechoslovakia a week later and Jews were beaten senseless on German city streets as their shops were looted during Kristallnacht we began to have second thoughts. Belatedly, air raid precautions were undertaken in earnest. Bomb shelters, like this one being opened by the mayor in tunnels under Chestergate, Stockport that held 4,000 people, were fitted out. Anderson shelters, named after the Home Secretary, appeared on waste land and in back gardens and gas masks were issued in an attempt to bolster our defences to attack. The Air Raid Wardens' service had been created in 1937 and the Women's Voluntary Service in 1938, but initial response to these and similar organisations was slow amongst the apathetic British. However, when reality dawned the civil defence units received a flood of volunteers.

Below: Parties of Manchester school children and their teachers board buses on the first stage of their evacuation. The scene was echoed in cities around the country as the nationwide evacuation operation got underway on 1st September 1939. Labelled like packages, and just as impersonally, the children were dispatched to the clean air and safety of the countryside. Four thousand special trains were laid on for the evacuation of school age children, mothers with toddlers and young babies, and the operation went off with clockwork precision. Like soldiers on military exercises none of them were told where they were going.

They arrived at their destination dirty, tired, bewildered and unhappy, and were picked out by householders or assigned to families by officers who had the authority to compel householders to billet a child. Some of the children were contented enough with their new way of life, but others wrote imploring their mothers to come and take them home. A few months later almost half the children had returned to the city. Others also left the danger zones. Civil servants were removed to small and quiet towns; some departments of the BBC moved to Worcester, and the Bank of England relocated to Hampshire.

Above: When it came to civil defence Britain had to rely on a variety of ordinary people to take over duties that would normally have been the remit of hardened professionals. Air Raid Precautions (ARP) were handed over to civilians, some of whom were in reserved occupations but also included a large number who were too young, too old or the wrong gender to be called up into the armed forces. This member of Salford's ARP was a young woman willing to put her own life on the line in the interests of the country. She pedalled her bicycle furiously around the streets advising householders to observe the blackout, waving a rattle or blowing a whistle to warn of an air raid and remaining at her post as bombs exploded around her, waiting for an opportunity to go and assist the rescue teams. When our young people showed such courage and dedication it is little wonder that we pulled through, despite everything that Hitler chose to throw at us. The Duke of Kent must have been impressed with that steely look of determination she showed when being presented to him in 1941. He was the husband of Princess Marina of Greece and father of the present Duke, Princess Alexandra and Prince Michael. His life ended tragically in a flying accident the following year.

Below: War had been declared, and every citizen of Britain, young and old, male and female, was called upon to put his or her back into the war effort. Those who did not go into military service of one kind or another worked in factories, dug for victory, gave up their aluminium baths and saucepans, joined organisations and aided in any way they could. These boys from Manchester Grammar School were not going to be left out; they might be too young to fight but while there were sandbags to be filled they were going to do their bit to protect their school building. Thousands of sandbags were used during World War II to protect the city's Victorian heritage and its beautiful civic buildings.

Manchester Grammar School has a long and illustrious history. Founded back in 1515 as the Manchester Free Grammar School, the school has an impressive record of student success, and many of Britain's leading academics and successful businessmen began their student life within its walls. The school abandoned its premises in Long Millgate in 1931, moving out of the city to Fallowfield. The move proved to be fortuitous; a German bomb put paid to the Long Millgate buildings in 1940.

Right: It was 1939, and Prime Minister Neville Chamberlain had made his announcement to the waiting people of Britain that '…this country is at war with Germany.' Manchester along with the rest of the country rolled up its sleeves and prepared for the inevitable. This war would be different from other wars. This time planes had the ability to fly further and carry a heavier load, and air raids were fully expected. Air raid shelters were obviously going to be needed, and the photograph shows a wooden framework being erected in Albert Square that was to form the basis for the surface shelters. Similar shelters were built on open places across the city, and older Mancunians will remember that they were indeed

needed when the expected air raids were made. One became an unexpected labour ward when a woman gave birth to a baby in an air raid shelter in 1940. Other preparations were hastily made. Place names and other identifying marks were obliterated to confuse the enemy about exactly where they were. Notices went up everywhere giving good advice to citizens on a number of issues. 'Keep Mum - she's not so dumb' warned people to take care what kind of information they passed on, as the person they were speaking to could be an enemy.

Below: This Manchester trolleybus found itself a victim of the 1941 blitz when it was caught while in service by the blast from a high explosive bomb, making its smart red and white livery look decidedly the worse for wear. But Number 1081, brought into service in 1938, was repaired and served Manchester well until it was withdrawn and scrapped in 1951. It was one of a number of buses damaged during the war. Manchester bus operators had a tough time of it during the war. Many of their staff enlisted in the services and women stepped in to replace them where possible. There were other dilemmas to face. Spare parts were like gold dust and were just as elusive. For example, from a total of 225 buses owned by Salford Corporation in 1945 only 169 were usable, and many of those needed urgent maintenance. Yet petrol rationing, coupled with more people commuting to factories, meant that more were using public transport. The blackout too caused problems, and drivers had to learn to 'feel' their way around the city streets, while inside the lights were so dim that the unfortunate conductresses scarcely knew whether they were being given a halfpenny or a shilling.

Above: The first few days of September 1939 were sad days for parents and children alike as Manchester schoolchildren were evacuated from the city. Evacuation to a place of safety was a wise move; in the early days of World War II many children from other parts of the country were even shipped abroad. But even so it must have been heartbreaking for the kiddies who were taken away from their mothers and families. Many had already said goodbye to fathers (some of them for the last time) who had already signed up for military service. It surely took great courage on the part of the parents of these children, to see them packed off to other parts of the country where they would be put into the care of strangers. Some would be fortunate, and be given a place where they would find love and real T.L.C. as part of another family. Others less lucky found themselves lost and lonely, billeted with people who did not like or understand children. The children were given a list of clothing and other items they had to take with them. The all important gas mask came at the top of the list.

Above: 'If the gas rattles sound, put your gas mask on at once, even in bed,' government leaflets instructed the people of Britain during the Second World War. Mustard gas attacks had been feared, and 38 million masks had been distributed as early as 1938. But by 1940 gas fears receded and few people bothered to carry them around any more. When war broke out every effort was made to accustom children to the frightening and claustrophobic gas masks that made parents and friends look like fearsome monsters. This photograph was taken at St Joseph's police premises in Longsight. The little boy on the left looks quite relaxed and confident wearing his mask, though the boy on the right of the picture doesn't seem quite so sure. Children had regular half hour gas mask drills in local community halls. Once they had got used to the strange look of the masks children found the occasions quite exciting. The masks when new were very stiff and tight, and were uncomfortable to wear. After a while they grew comfortable - then along would come an official who would test it, declare it unsafe and issue another quite safe but very uncomfortable mask!

Above: The city prepares for war, and these young girls from Sharston Senior School look remarkably cheerful as they practise their air raid precautions. But then, the reality of war was still a future experience not to be realised until the blitz of 1940-41. The girls' thoughts were perhaps dwelling on happier subjects as they queued up that rainy day, gas masks over their shoulders, to enter the school's air raid shelter. The threat of gas was a very real one; many of these girls' grandfathers would have suffered from the deadly, all pervasive mustard gas used by the enemy during World War I. So, at least at the outset of World War II, the nation dutifully carried its gas masks everywhere. As the war went on and gas was not used, the masks themselves were as often as not left behind as ladies found the cases just right for carrying lipstick, rouge and a powder compact, and men discovered that a packet of sandwiches would fit nicely into them.

Bottom, facing page: Bombs fell indiscriminately during the Second World War, and hospitals and nurses' homes were added to the list of bombed out buildings, often with casualties and sadly, fatalities. Some buses were equipped with their own supply of stretchers; perhaps the one in the photograph was one of them? The vehicles would have been used to transfer hospital patients from areas of danger, and the picture shows a small patient being carefully moved from (or into?) the bus via the rear window. Not an ideal exit, but 'where there's a will, there's a way'. The will was certainly there, and the way was obvious. There are records of real heroism by hospital staff; doctors and nurses evacuated a ward full of teenagers when their hospital was hit by high explosive bombs, one of the nurses was herself injured in the raid.

Below: This Leyland Lion bus was given a different and very worthy job to do during World War II. Used by the Air Raid Prevention as a First Aid Post, the vehicle could be quickly moved to the location of any emergency; as quickly, that is, as the state of the roads would allow. Piles of rubble blocking thoroughfares meant that ambulances and public transport faced many detours and could rarely use the same route around the city every day. The nursing staff, often seen as angels in uniform, were on the scene as quickly as possible, however, after an air raid, ready to save lives, bandage injuries and comfort those who had found themselves suddenly homeless. First Aid Posts were set up in many unusual places such as hotels and schools to treat the victims of bomb damage.

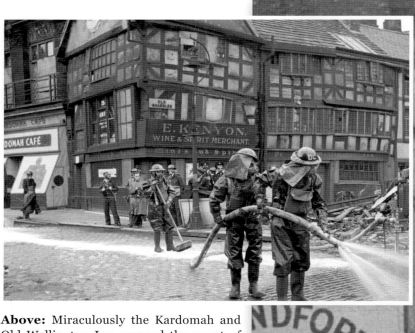

Above: Miraculously the Kardomah and Old Wellington Inn escaped the worst of the damage caused by the bombing raids on Manchester in December 1940, though the rest of Old Shambles and Market Place was devastated. The attacks left Manchester's fire service so stretched that 200 firemen had to be brought in from Liverpool to lend assistance. The Cathedral, Free Trade Hall, Exchange station and Victoria Station were just a handful of the major buildings that were either gutted or badly damaged. Some 30,000 houses were destroyed and further raids in January 1941 hit Trafford Park, followed by other notable attacks in June 1941 that brought serious loss of life. The defence workers seen here in Market Place were members of a decontamination squad. Their gas masks and protective clothing were necessary guards against the possibilities of infection and disease as they hosed down the cobbles that might have contained noxious substances that sadly might have included blood and body parts. There was also an outside chance that some of the bombs that fell might have included poison gas or bacteria that could have been even more harmful than the tons of high explosive. In 1971 the Old Wellington was jacked up and moved to its present site in Exchange Square on the edge of the Arndale Centre during redevelopment work that completely changed the nature of this part of the city.

The city centre was hammered by the aerial bombardments of the second world war. Trafford Park was a vital part of the country's war machine with its engineering and aircraft manufacturing plants, especially those of MetroVickers. The production of the Lancaster bomber and radar equipment and the large arsenal here, in addition to the nearby oil terminal, made Manchester a prime target for enemy action. A major assault was launched late in 1940 when, in the three nights leading up to Christmas, incendiaries and high explosive set the city on fire and reduced much of the centre to rubble. In the first night of the raids 233 bombs exploded during a five hour period of terror that destroyed or damaged nearly everything within a one mile radius of Albert Square. A huge proportion of Manchester's commercial and historic wealth was wiped off the map in that short space of time. The aftermath in Market Place showed the carnage that had been brought to this once attractive old quarter. The Corn Exchange was damaged, but still stood overlooking the piles of bricks and fallen masonry underneath the shadow of its dome. In 1903 it had replaced the previous 1837 building on Hanging Ditch at a cost of £350,000. Censorship rules meant that the bombing was initially reported as affecting a 'town in the northwest', but anyone living within 20 miles of the city could have identified it from the glow in the night sky.

The Crusader tank bowling along Princess Street in 1942 was part of a morale boosting and fund raising exercise for the war effort. It was a sight that impressed the large crowd that turned out to witness the event. Hardly a month seemed to pass by without some appeal being made to the nation's generosity. There was Warship Week, Spitfire Week and Wastepaper Week, all dedicated to the cause of encouraging us to give what we could to help win the war. Some remarkable feats of recycling took place as pots and pans, old railings and rusty nails reappeared above our heads as a fighter plane or set sail as a destroyer bound for the open seas.

Some towns raised money to adopt their own tanks and thermometers were erected on town halls to chart the progress of cash flowing in to swell the coffers. Old curtains, rags and clothing were collected by the Women's Voluntary Service and were restyled as parachutes or uniforms. There seemed no end to the imagination of those in charge of scouring the country for anything that might be remotely useful. Britain became a land of hoarders as families never threw anything away for fear that they would be accused of being wasteful and all the time we turned our back gardens into mini allotments as we dug for victory.

Above: Although some buildings nearby escaped virtually unscathed there was no reprieve for the Free Trade Hall as it suffered a dreadful beating from the attacks from above on 23 December 1940. Edward Waters designed this famous Peter Street building and work on it began in 1853. Having cost £40,000 the official opening ceremony took place on 10 October 1856. Originally called Manchester Guild Hall, it had a seating capacity of 3,165 and was one of the city's major centres. It lay as but a shell for the rest of the war but was restored to its former glory and reopened by Queen Elizabeth in 1951 in one of the last public engagements she performed before being sadly widowed the following February. The Free Trade Hall has hosted a variety of events, ranging from religious meetings to wrestling and from exhibitions to school speech days. In the early 20th century suffragettes held rallies within its walls and a variety of political philosophies have been heard echoing from its stage over the intervening years. However, for most people the Free Trade Hall will forever be associated with the orchestra named for Charles Hallé, the first principal of the Royal Manchester College of Music. Under the baton of John Barbirolli, conductor from 1943 to 1968, the HallÈ continued and perhaps surpassed the reputation built up during Hans Richter's time as its conductor at the start of the century.

Above: The big wigs were out in force in what was left of the Royal Exchange in early 1941. They had come to view the damage caused in the previous month's air raid. Included in the official party were the Home Secretary and King George VI, but it was Queen Elizabeth who was taking the lead as they viewed the wreckage of the third Royal Exchange in Manchester's history. This building was erected in 1874 and, after being enlarged, was reopened by George V in October 1921. During the war Queen Elizabeth was often at the forefront of such scenes

as she guided her nervous husband through his royal duties. Born Elizabeth Bowes-Lyon in 1900, she had little expected to be thrust so far into the limelight, even when she married the Duke of York in 1923. When her brother-in-law, Edward VIII, abdicated in 1936 and her husband stepped into the breach, she helped him take the reins by involving herself as no previous consort had done before. The couple endeared themselves to the general public by refusing to slip away to a safe haven in Canada and stayed at home to brave the dangers of aerial bombardment just like the rest of us. This was supposed to be a secret visit, but word soon got out and before long wellwishers arrived to give the royal couple a rousing cheer.

Below: That some famous and historic buildings survived the air raids was just a matter of luck. The Midland Hotel, Town Hall, Central Library and Art Gallery somehow managed to avoid the fate that befell so many others that were reduced to burnt out shells or became just so many piles of rubble. The aftermath left a pall of acrid smoke and brick dust hanging over the city as though it were some sort of relation to the industrial smogs that bedevilled residents until the 1950s. Workmen sifting through the debris were surprised to see King George VI arrive for his own personal assessment of the damage. Quite what the bobby on the left was guarding is difficult to fathom as little of value had been left intact and, thankfully, we were not a nation of looters. We were more likely to salvage something on behalf of a neighbour than keep it for ourselves. Wartime was a horrid experience but there really was an atmosphere of bonding and togetherness in the struggle against a common foe. To see the King take an interest was a firm morale booster.

STREETS OF CHANGE

were just as bad. Little wonder that the 1930s brought in driving tests, Belisha pedestrian crossings, Percy Shaw's cats' eyes and more widespread electrically operated traffic lights. Road safety education came too late for one famous figure when TE Lawrence, of Arabia fame, was killed in a motor cycle crash in May that year.

Right: 1946 is the date of this fascinating old photograph, and Victoria Street appears to be full of jay walkers. A crossing with Belisha beacons has been provided, but nobody is using it. All the cars in the picture are pre war, even though it is a year since the end of World War II. Post war prosperity, when most families will own their own car, has yet to come to the ordinary working Mancunian, and in the meantime public transport is the more usual way of getting about. Even so there are a number of interesting, not to say illustrious, vehicles about. One can almost smell the fine leather of the comfortable upholstered interior of the Rolls Royce in the right foreground. The large and sleek upper class saloon ahead is from the other side of the Atlantic, possibly a Chrysler or a Bewick, drawing the eye to its unusual silver grey colour. A Number 16 bus (possibly wearing Salford livery?) is giving way to the horse and cart crossing the intersection; the city still had a large number of working horses during the 1940s. Coming the other way is one of Manchester's last trams, built in 1929-30 and known as 'Pilcher' cars.

Below: Cobbled carriageways, tram tracks and black saloon cars heading down from Piccadilly take Portland Street back to 1935 when Europe was about to experience turmoil once more. At home we seemed more concerned with the retirement of Jack Hobbs, England's greatest batsman, or Malcolm Campbell smashing the 300 mph land speed barrier in Bluebird. The League of Ovaltineys praising hot, milky bedtime drinks was more in our minds than warnings or warmongering put out by the League of Nations. As you can see from this picture the lack of road safety measures was becoming an issue on our roads. Compared with the number of vehicles that we had the road accident statistics were quite horrific. As can be seen here, pedestrians took their life in their hands as they braved the traffic to cross the street. Out in the suburbs or more rural areas things

Below: Seen in 1939 from the station approach, Oxford Street's Palace Theatre had been in business for nearly half a century ever since it admitted its first paying customers during Whit week in 1891. It had originally been intended as a Palace of City Varieties but there had been a groundswell of Methodist mentality that objected to popular music hall and all that was associated with that style of entertainment. Influential figures railed against the culture of alcohol and dubious morality that seemed to accompany both the entertainers and their public, labelling all involved as drunks or degenerates or both. However a programme of grand ballet and similar artistic productions meant that the Palace could open without upsetting those who took the moral high ground, but for many years the theatre was denied a drinks licence. Once under way more middle of the road shows were put on and Little Tich, Dan Leno, Marie Lloyd and George Formby Senior all trod the Palace boards. Charlie Chaplin was on the bill in 1903 as the Palace went from strength to strength. By the middle of the last century it had gained a reputation for conventional drama, offering touring companies the opportunity to present productions. Many readers will also recall the fabulous pantomimes without which the Christmas season was not complete. The theatre closed in 1978 but reopened in 1981 after major refurbishment.

Right: This 1946 picture was taken from up high on the Central Library roof, to look across St Peter's Square and along Oxford Street towards the Palace Theatre that stands on the corner of Whitworth Street. It was a time to start the process of restoring both buildings and shattered dreams. That would not be easy and we remembered how difficult life was after the previous conflict when jobs were scarce and the war debt that accrued bit into the economy. It was not as if the whole world was at peace again. There was terrorism in Palestine and religious rioting in India, but the most worrying development came to our notice when America tested an atomic bomb at Bikini atoll in the Pacific. At home there was a flourishing black market in nylons, chocolates, perfume and other scarce commodities. Crime was on the increase again and the man in the street was not as confident of a rosy future as he had been on VE Day. Then he had stood near the Cenotaph in St Peter's Square to celebrate the end of the war and remember those who had fallen. This memorial, designed by Lutyens and originally intended for Albert Square, was not consecrated until 1924, having been delayed by the withholding of royal assent for moving the Albert Memorial. The cross on the left marks the site of the altar of the old St Peter's church.

Below: The little railway bridge is alongside Oxford Road station as we look towards Oxford Street and the Palace Theatre. The Oxford Road station is at the junction of Whitworth Street West and Oxford Street, on an elevated track between Deansgate and Piccadilly stations. It was opened on 20 July, 1849, by Manchester South Junction and Altrincham Railway. On the right is the Victorian terracotta Refuge Assurance buildings. Situated just off the city centre on Oxford Street opposite the Palace Theatre and

across from the Cornerhouse and Oxford Road Station, this fabulous building, formerly the Charterhouse Hotel, now part of the Le Meridien hotels chain, has been resurrected after standing idle for a few years, since its original occupants, the Refuge Insurance Company vacated it. The Palace Hotel is a recognised landmark of Manchester, thanks to its distinctive 217ft tall clock tower. Still known locally (and with good reason) as the 'Refuge Building', it is a distinctive landmark to visitors approaching Manchester from the south. This Grade II Listed Building is one of the city's best Victorian structures. The photographer was standing opposite where the BBC TV studio can now be found, with Charles Street to the right.

Below: Manchester Cathedral, seen in the distance, dates from a structure erected in the 15th century, though there had been places of worship there before. Somewhat detached now from the main City Centre, by virtue of its riverside location, the cathedral marked the epicentre of medieval Manchester. Today's

Manchester Cathedral has taken 600 years in the making. It was extensively renovated on several occasions in the 19th century and its 130 foot tower rebuilt in 1887. The new Lady Chapel was created during repairs needed after the cathedral was badly damaged by the 1940 bombing. Deansgate in 1950 was very quiet, but car ownership was not widespread and fuel was still in short supply. There must have been something very eyecatching in Vivian Grant's window as several heads have turned to have a good look. Above them was lettering promoting pianos and radios. It was still popular to have a piano in your drawing room, even if no one could play it properly, as it was a sign that the family came from a cultured and sophisticated background despite a lack of obvious wealth. A radio was an essential piece of equipment for both information and entertainment. The Home programme brought the news and serious drama and the Light gave us 'Much Binding in the Marsh' and 'ITMA', though we rather drew the line at a turgid Mahler symphony on the Third programme.

Above: Petrol was still at a premium and car ownership not on a widespread scale in c1950, but it hardly appeared to be so in Albert Square as witnessed by the line of parked cars. Shops have replaced the Scottish Provident buildings that towered above the trams on the left, but the Northern Assurance Buildings on the right can still be seen on Princess Street. The trolley bus wires were taken away in the mid 1960s, but the rest of the scene is immediately recognisable. The Albert Memorial is the centre piece of the city's heartland, having stood here for 140 years. Prince Albert, the beloved husband of Queen Victoria, died unexpectedly in 1861 and all across the country memorial parks and statues appeared to mark his place in Her Majesty's affections. Albert Square was created specifically for this reason. Originally it had been intended to erect a memorial in Piccadilly, but the Infirmary was not keen to surrender some of its land in this cause. As an alternative, slums and the land around Town Yard were cleared with the demolition of over 100 buildings, to provide space for the memorial and the creation of the new Town Hall. The previous centre of administration had been on King Street, but the accommodation was too small after Manchester became a city in 1853 and the demands upon local government increased. In April 1972, the Albert Square area was designated a conservation area, and this was extended in 1981 to include the neighboring, newly created Lincoln Square. (The creation of Lincoln Square completed a "processional way" from the Law Courts through Spinningfield and Lincoln Square to the Town Hall.)

Below: Since opening in 1755 the Royal Infirmary was the main building in this area that was developed from what was once an old clay pit. After the hospital's closure in 1908 and subsequent demolition Piccadilly Gardens were developed as an idyllic green oasis in the centre of the city where the housing around about was being replaced by hotels and commercial buildings. The bus terminus was opened on the edge of Piccadilly and now serves modern trams as well. This open view of Piccadilly Gardens is one to savour as it has been affected by the craze for high rise structures over the last 40 years. Piccadilly Plaza, that concrete slab of a place, began to raise its controversial face well above the skyline in 1959 and it took until 1965 to complete the hotel and office blocks. The demand for building more and more developments continues into this century as the Argent Group remodels the area known as the Piccadilly Triangle. That will include an office block and car park on the gardens that will be remodelled, but can never again recapture the serenity of the scene that was photographed in 1953. Then they looked so pretty as decorations were prepared to celebrate the coronation of Queen Elizabeth II. As we got ready to enjoy the moment little did we know of the concrete shadow that was soon to fall across Piccadilly Gardens.

to take in what this Pythagoras chap had been on about with his squares, sides and something about a hypotenuse. We had enough to worry about with clausal analysis, trying to determine whether these words made up an adverbial or adjectival clause. What did we do with it when we discovered what it was and has anyone ever found a use in real life for finding out the length of a ladder leaning against a wall or the height of a tree from the shadow it cast upon the ground? The Duke of Devonshire opened the magnificent new building in 1900 as the Whitworth Street School until 1904. Renamed Manchester Municipal Secondary School it was extremely popular and an extension was completed in 1911. At the outbreak of the Great War in 1914, the building was converted to a military hospital. Pupils - both boys and girls - returned to the newly-named Central High School in 1920. This identity remained until 1960, although the boys had left in 1954. It was appropriate at this time to re-name the school Central High School for Girls. Following Manchester educational re-organisation of 1982, the building became home to Shena Simon College.

Top: In 1958 the Clarendon Hotel on Oxford Road was still part of the culture largely dominated by mature males. Pubs were places where you could escape from work or the missus and enjoy a pint or two with pals and put the world to rights. Earnest conversations about the fortunes of United and City took place without any satisfactory conclusion ever being reached. The government of the day was pulled to pieces, but still returned to power in the next election. Club 43 was housed in the Clarendon Hotel and Joe Palin, who died aged 73, was arguably the best bebop pianist to come out of Manchester. In 1956 he became the house pianist of Club 43, playing with various London artists, among them Tubby Hayes, Ronnie Scott and Don Rendell. Demolished during construction of the Mancunian Way, the Clarendon's site is now occupied by a flyover on Oxford Road.

Right: Were they the best days of our lives? The teachers at Manchester Central High School for Girls on Whitworth Street would have had us think so, but we were too busy living life to the full to dwell on such prissy statements. Anyway, it was hardly memorable sitting in class in 1958 trying

Below: This cinema on Market Street next to Yates' Wine Lodge was called the Cinephone. It showed mainly french and italian films which were a little more racey than the usual british and american films of the time. On this day in 1957 the main attraction advertised was an italian comedy film called 'Scandal in Sorrento', starring Sophia Loren an Vittorio De Sica. Sophia Loren, born Sophia Villani Scicolone in Rome on 20 September, 1934, was beginning to make a name for herself in leading roles that emphasised her voluptuous figure. Cinephone described itself as Manchester's continental cinema showing art films which were the X certificate movies that left very little to the imagination. However, as shown by the clock on Henry's building it's obviously a bit too early for the 'Midnight Movie'. It all seems silly and tame to us in the 21st century when the content of modern television programmes can be far more lurid than anything on offer in the Cinephone, but at the time the fare on offer was eye opening in every sense.

Above: Corporation Street was constructed in 1845, running from its corner here with Market Street out to the north towards Collyhurst. In 1958 buildings were being created to host new or extended businesses, either by renovating sites or finishing off the last of the regeneration work from the postwar years. Whilst all the work continued around it Burton's carried on its traditional trade as a men's outfitter. Meshe Minsky, a Lithuanian Jew, changed his name to Montague Burton when he came to Chesterfield in 1900. By 1910 he had opened four shops and as his empire grew he moved his headquarters to a large factory site in Leeds and from there and his Harrogate home by the 1930s he was opening an outlet in a new town on a monthly basis. There were many rivals in his line of business and Hepworth's, Weaver to Wearer, Dunn's and Fifty Shilling Tailors all had their supporters. Slogans helped catch the public's imagination, as with John Collier's 'the window to watch', but Burton's was 'the tailor of taste'. The cranes

swinging above Burton's in 1958 returned with a vengeance in the early 1970s when the Arndale Centre was begun. By the time of its completion in 1979 it had changed both the face and the shopping style of this part of the city. Over 200 shops were accommodated within its 30 acre site.

Inset: Poet Rupert Brooke was thinking of a vicarage in Grantchester when he asked 'Is there honey still for tea?' His romantic view of this land of ours was written nearly 50 years before this photograph of the Old Shambles in Market Place was taken in 1958, but the visions his words conjured up could have been applied to this little oasis of tradition. The building known as the Old Wellington Inn dates from at least as far back as 1550 and adopted its name as a pub in 1830. How popular a title that was in its early days is difficult to imagine since the Duke of Wellington, despite being a hero of Waterloo, was reviled in many quarters because of his association with the Peterloo massacre. Rupert Brooke's honey might have been available for serving in the Kardomah Café, a gentle haven for ladies of certain years to sip elegantly from their teacups whilst criticising the world around them. They tut-tutted about the drainpipe trousers and luminous socks worn by young men going past the window and despaired about the gyrations of someone called Elvis who it seemed was rocking in a jailhouse. 'Pity they did not throw away the key,' one was heard to remark. Their tranquility was occasionally interrupted by a waitress shouting, 'Egg on a barm!' as she passed an order to the kitchen down a voice tube. Another branch of Kardomah was situated in St Ann's Square and is now a McDonald's.

Top: Zorro, the masked adventurer and righter of wrongs, was just one of the characters about whom we fantasised as children. Having seen a film in which he appeared we made cardboard shapes to which we attached a bit of elastic and wrapped them across our eyes. With a piece of wood doubling as a duelling sword, off we went slashing away madly at invisible opponents. On other occasions we came back home from the Saturday matinee full of excitement at the predicament in which Flash Gordon had been left in his latest cliffhanger when his rocket, trailing sparks behind it, had crashlanded on some remote planet and was left dangling over a precipice. We knew he would escape, but now had to be left until next week. By 1961 the Empress on Oldham Road, Miles Platting was beginning to show its age. Its earlier glories would eventually be lost to the dreaded scourge of bingo and stands now as a throwback to the days when this was a busy and thriving part of Manchester, with a large local population who lived and worked here. It opened in 1912 as the Empress Electric Theatre in the very early days of purpose-built cinemas. Its now somewhat forlorn facade of red Accrington brick harks back to the 19th century, giving it an industrial appearance but with almost castle-like cornice adornments to its pyramid shape.

Above: The little lad leading the way across the Princess Street zebra crossing in 1961 will be in his mid-50 by now. Can he remember what it was like to wear short trousers and have chapped legs in the winter time and permanent scabs on his knees from playground falls during a 25 a side game of soccer? Head down he was then thinking about the Biggles book that he had got out of the library and was anxious to lose himself in the WE Johns' plot of daring do, chocks away and camaraderie with Archie and Ginger. Tucked away under a cushion on the sofa was a copy of the Eagle with more adventure in the shape of Dan Dare, or perhaps he had other comics like the Hotspur, Rover or Wizard. Great stories awaited him when Limpalong Leslie overcame his handicap to score the winning goal, Alf Tupper ran along the track on a diet of faggots and peas and the mighty Wilson won the Ashes singlehandedly. It was grand to be a boy in 1961. There were seasons for conkers and marbles and girls to be teased. Dens were to be made out of old mattresses and bits of wood on the spare ground at the back of Auntie Muriel's house. She was not a real relative, but every child called a neighbour auntie or uncle 40 years ago.

Next door to the Café Royal on Peter Street the last film reels turned in the projection room of the Gaiety in June 1959 when the main feature, 'Al Capone', included a fine performance by Rod Steiger as the infamous Chicago gangster in this semi documentary style of movie. The cinema began life as the Gaiety Theatre of Varieties in 1878 on the site of an old circus. It burned down five years later and was rebuilt at a cost of £15,000 as the Comedy Theatre, reopening on 22 December 1884. It held 1,500 and was renamed the Gaiety Theatre in 1903 and prided itself on being something out of the ordinary, as instanced by some of the high admission charges. Even those in the wealthy middle classes blinked when asked for two guineas for the privilege of sitting in a private box. The Gaiety succumbed to the increased demand for picture palaces after World War I and made the switch from stage to screen in May 1921. There was some attempt to revive music hall and pantomime in the 1930s but with minimal success. The attractions of Hollywood were all too powerful and the record breaking 54 week run of 'Gone with the Wind' proved that audiences of the day had turned their back on old style entertainment. After the cinema's closure the site was cleared in August 1959 and Television House appeared in its stead.

obbled streets, back yards and terraced housing provided the backdrop for 'Coronation Street', the longrunning TV soap opera that was first screened in 1960, two years before these lads posed for the camera. The story lines in the early days typified life in the industrial north and concentrated on old dears like Ena, Martha and Minnie supping their milk stout in the snug. Women wore curlers under a headscarf and decorated their living rooms with flying ducks on the wall. The children played with whatever they could lay their hands on. These boys could have turned the cart into a chariot from the 'Ben Hur' movie they might have been lucky enough to see. On another day it would have been a stagecoach in which they rode with John Wayne, firing off imaginary six-shooters at outlaws or a covered wagon driven by Ward Bond's Seth Adams in 'Wagon Train'. In the latter case the lads imagined that it was part of a circle of such prairie schooners from which they could fight off an attack by Red Indians. Their private world was shattered when the window cleaner returned and told them to get off his cart, but then they had other things to which they could turn their attention. A battered old tennis ball, missing most of its outer fur, was produced and they had an enjoyable game of wall-y, kicking the ball against the brickwork as they honed the skills that might see Joe Armstrong or some other soccer scout give them the nod in years to come.

Right: In 1962 little children could play happily, whatever their surroundings. They are never more content than when messing about with old treasures that they have found. To them an old abandoned chair and a few other assorted bits and pieces can provide the basis for a den, something to call their own. Imaginations can run wild as they turn the most unlikely discoveries and inhospitable terrain into something in which they can lose themselves for a few hours, wrapped up in their own little world. If they came home at the end of the day with dirty faces and grubby knees then that was sure proof of the fun they had. These back yards and derelict sites in Hulme were gradually cleared as part of a slum clearance project and many of the families were rehoused in Wythenshawe or the other newly designated townships that developed in the suburbs to receive new populations. Hyde, Worsley, Heywood and the Langley estate in Middleton all received their share of new residents as 90,000 homes were demolished in a 20 year improvement programme that began in the mid 1950s. Tower blocks that appeared in Hulme proved to be socially disastrous and by the early 1990s many of these had been demolished to make way for a newer style of low level architecture.

Bottom: No look at Manchester would be complete without a visit to Coronation Street. The TV soap began in 1960 and is still near the top of the ratings almost 50 years later. The film set near Granada studios has become one of the major tourist attractions in the city, but there are a number of real Coronation Streets in Manchester and some of them provided the inspiration for the original idea behind the successful programme. This one in Openshaw was photographed in 1964 and shows the typical terraced housing in which so many of us were brought up. There was a true sense of community and, although everyone knew each other's business, a real togetherness existed. Even so, mums were fiercely protective of their own families and even the best of friends could fall out if a child was the victim of some perceived injustice at the hands of another. They ruled the roost and dad tipped up his pay packet each week as his wife doled out money into tins for the rent man, electricity, Christmas club, shopping etc before giving him back his beer and baccy money. Each street had its own particular characters, the grumpy granddad, the flighty piece at number 19 or the stuck up lah-de-dah with net curtains and a son who had passed his 11 plus.

Above: The cars have moved out and the cranes have moved in, and the notice by the gate of what was by this time a construction site reminds drivers that as from the 19th April 1960 the Piccadilly car park would be closed. Many readers will remember the city's famous square the way it looked back in 1960; the workmen's sheds that sprouted like mushrooms, the piles of equipment, the huge tower cranes lifting heavy blocks into position, the noise, the bustle - and here and there a few bars of the latest popular song whistled by a passing builder. And was it all worth it? The resulting Plaza Suite was controversial from the very start of its life; some loved it, a lot more hated it, but at least nobody ignored it.

Nearly forty years on the Hotel Piccadilly with the Plaza Cafe below, the Sunley Tower office block and Bernard House are showing their age and looking decidedly the worse for wear. Why is it that the modern 1960s 'angular block' developments seem to age faster than the timeless old Victorian buildings?

Right: Pedestrians pick their way gingerly around road works in Piccadilly in 1957 as more changes were made to the square. In the last hundred years or so Piccadilly has seen more changes than most places, yet incredibly is still recognisable in spite of its fringe of modern angular buildings. Younger Mancunians can scarcely visualise the square without its gardens, and many of them would be surprised to learn that the Manchester Royal Infirmary once stood on the site. The Infirmary, which included a 'lunatic asylum', was built in 1755 and dominated Piccadilly, the clock on its dome a well known landmark. The building has all but passed from living memory today, but the Infirmary served the citizens of Manchester well until it was demolished in 1908. Even during the process of demolition an accident and emergency room was kept open in Parker Street. King Edward VII opened the new Royal Infirmary out on the Oxford Road in 1909.

With the sun on their backs two elegant ladies strolled around Boggart Hole Clough in the summer of 1935 as scores of others sat enjoying the fine weather and indulging in polite conversation. The baby in the pram was screened from the worst of the rays by a pretty canopy as her mother or nanny took the weight off her feet in this idyllic spot in north Manchester, several miles out from the city centre. It is the third largest park within the council boundaries and its valleys, cloughs and hills cover some 190 acres. The park is probably Manchester's most interesting leisure area as it balances the scenic delights of steep ravines and sloping gullies with the attractions of activities that include a boating lake, soccer pitches and an athletics track. An annual firework display is also very popular. Boggart Hole Clough is, in some ways, like Liverpool's Knotty Ash as many people think that they are fictitious place names. The comedian Ken Dodd confused many with his talk of Diddymen in Knotty Ash jam butty mines and a Radio Two disc jockey, the late Ray Moore, did the same with his references to Boggart Hole Clough on his early morning show. There are many tales about exactly what the word 'boggart' means, but most are centred around a ghostly spectre that haunted a farmer's family.

AT LEISURE

Above: This is Whitworth Street's Ritz ballroom in 1930 where you could even hire a professional partner to help you enjoy an evening tripping the light fantastic. Until the beat groups came along and little dance clubs began to replace the large ballrooms, this was the face of dancing to popular music. There were crazes, just as in the 1960s when teenagers shook to the rhythm of the Twist, the Locomotion, the Funky Chicken and the Slosh, but between the wars they were the Black Bottom, the Charleston and the Lambeth Walk. But the most enduring steps were those danced to old ballroom favourites, the waltz, quickstep and foxtrot, with the more adventurous attempting the Latin American samba, rumba and cha-cha. Learning to dance properly was a social necessity for being unable to take the floor was decidedly infra dig. Many learned to at Tommy Rogers' studio on Oxford Road or in one of the host of smaller establishments in the suburbs. Painter's still ran a flourishing business in Urmston long after the Beatles held sway. The music in the dance halls did not come from a DJ scratching away on a turntable but from live bands, usually with a lead singer up front. Many famous solo artists cut their eyeteeth in big bands under the leadership of Jack Hylton, Jack Payne, Harry Roy or Joe Loss. Some bands, though, kept their singers with them for years and Billy Cotton's show would not have seemed the same without Kathy Kay or Alan Breeze on vocals.

Above: Getting away from the hustle and bustle of Deansgate to spend a lunch hour near the river in Parsonage Gardens always has been a good idea on a nice sunny day. These office workers in 1950 were glad to take a break from pounding the heavy keys of their manual Remington or Underwood qwerty keyboards. Their work was punctuated by the ping of a bell as the typewriter carriage nearly reached the end of its journey, prompting the typist to hit the handle of the carriage return ready to start a new line. Accuracy was very important because there was no such thing as cut and paste or a delete key as we have on modern computers and word processors. Make an error and it was start again as the boss had no time for erasers and correction fluid. The office of half a century ago was one of carbon paper, bulldog clips, filing cabinets and card indexes. Then there were the shorthand pads on which to take down dictation in Pitman shorthand we had learned at night school. A walk in the gardens was a release from all this and conversation turned to plans for next Saturday. A night at the Ritz ballroom, dancing to the big band sounds and catching the eye of some chap still wearing his demob suit was very likely, but we had to be back home by 11.30 or dad would have had something to say.

The bowler hats of the bank managers in their business suits, the flat caps of the working classes, the utility hats of the housewives and the jauntily angled headgear of the pretty young things all came together to share a moment in the sunshine gleaming down upon Piccadilly Gardens. The man in uniform, strolling around the path, would soon be demobbed as his job was almost done in the summer of 1945. Little Jimmy could go to sleep in his own little room again, as Vera Lynn told us, now that the bombs had stopped falling and he felt safe once more. During the war there were air raid shelters on Piccadilly Gardens, erected to provide some protection for shoppers and workers when the sirens sounded as they often did. Wardens were in place to lend a hand with the organisation, keeping the shelters open from 8 am to 7 pm. The gardens have long been an attractive place to while away a lunch hour and just close your eyes and forget the ticking off that the boss has just dished out. In 1945 it was also an opportunity to reflect upon the debt we owed to the likes of the uniformed serviceman walking around the gardens who had woken up each morning never knowing whether or not it was going to be his last.

Above: Alan Bates and June Ritchie, a new find, were the lovers in the 'X' rated movie 'A Kind of Loving' which was showing at the ABC Cinema in 1962. Thora Hird played June Ritchie's domineering middle class mother, who believed that Bates's character was not good enough for her daughter. The actor Alan Bates is remembered by most film buffs for his nude scenes in D H Lawrence's 'Women in Love', in which he starred with Glenda Jackson and Oliver Reed. The modern and popular Deansgate cinema opposite the Barton Arcade survived television and was a focal point for city centre cinema-goers until the 1980s - 90s. Sadly, falling audiences, possibly hastened on by the growing trend for renting films on video, brought about its demise. The building's use changed, and it is currently a popular pub, providing Mancunians with a night out and the liquid refreshment they need.

Left: Mancunians have always enjoyed a night out as much as anyone else, and the city has long offered them a bewildering choice of cinemas, pubs, clubs, dance halls and theatres. Remember the Gaumont? This dramatic photograph of the ultra-modern Gaumont Cinema in Oxford Street was taken in 1935, when the film 'The Rage of Paris', starring Douglas Fairbanks Junior, was being screened. Back in 1904 the old Hippodrome was providing entertainment for the citizens of Manchester on the same site. The Hippodrome ended its days around 1934/35, becoming the Ardwick Hippodrome. It was later redeveloped as a cinema and became the Gaumont. The building's yellow tiles were a fashionable feature of the day. The chocolate shop is nicely placed between the Gaumont and the New Oxford Theatre, and must have been very well patronised. The Gaumont came to a sad end, as many did across the city when the growing popularity of television badly affected cinema audiences, and the whole block was demolished.

Above: The Gaumont Cinema in Chorlton-cum-Hardy has a chequered history. Opening as the Majestic it then became the Savoy, next the Gaumont, then the ABC - and is currently an undertaker's parlour. The children in this 1958 photograph have just been to the Saturday matinee. These children's shows were great value for money, and for just a few coppers they could see one of the popular cartoons, a couple of feature films, and often a 'cliffhanger' serial that left the heroine tied to the railway line for a nail-biting week until next Saturday. In the meantime they would hope against hope that nothing would prevent them from finding out what happened to the luckless female - though deep down they knew full well that some super-hero would come along and rescue her in the nick of time. Between the films, exciting trailers of forthcoming films would entice them back time and again. The whole programme was, of course, punctuated by cheers and jeers, flying bits of rubbish, the popping of bubble gum, the 'oohs' of excitement, and the shouts of 'Put a penny in!' that harassed the long suffering projectionist when the film broke, as frequently happened. All very thrilling stuff.

Below: Belle Vue's elephants acted as a magnet for the kiddies, and for years hundreds of intrepid youngsters queued up to take a ride high above the ground on the swaying wooden seats carried on each side of the magnificent animal. The exotically dressed figure seen in the photograph with the elephant was Phil Fernandez; an unlikely name for the Malayan keeper who joined the team at Belle Vue's zoo as early as 1921, bringing with him his elephant Lil. It is quite possible that the elephant in this photograph is Lil herself. Fernandez was a familiar sight around the complex, always in the oriental robes that gave the attraction an aura of Eastern mystery. Lil was not the only elephant at Belle Vue; another was called Mary, and Annie was purchased from Sangers Circus in 1941 at a cost of 50 guineas. (Readers too young to remember guineas might like to know that a guinea was worth one pound and one shilling - £1.5p in today's currency.) Fernandez remained at Belle Vue and was in charge of the elephant rides until his own death in 1956. By that time a new children's zoo had been introduced at a cost of £15,000.

going (albeit with great difficulty) during World War II, though in the blitz of 1940 and 1941 only afternoon performances were possible. Most of the staff were, of course, fighting for king and country, and George Lockhart carried on single handedly all through the war. Lockhart, described as the 'Prince of Ringmasters', was a very able linguist, and his charm and charisma gave him instant rapport with audiences. His position as ringmaster gave him authority over all the acts and carried great responsibility. Lockhart went on working long after most men of his years had opted for a pipe and slippers, eventually retiring in 1972 at the amazing age of 90! His name lives on as a street name on one of Manchester's Wimpey housing estates.

Top right: You don't see a string of elephants parading around the streets of Manchester every day, and here the camera has captured the eager crowd of onlookers who gathered to watch the unusual sight. A circus was introduced to Belle Vue pleasure grounds as early as 1929, and was put in the sole charge of the well known Blackpool Tower ringmaster George Lockhart. The circus was one of the few Belle Vue attractions to be kept

Right: When Coronation Street arrived on Granada's TV schedules in 1960 it included a trio of characters who might have been modelled on the three women seen feeding the giraffes at Belle Vue Zoo in 1953. Ena, Minnie and Martha were representative of the bedrock of northern working class society, firm in their views and distrustful of change. As friends they were allowed to score points off each other, but fiercely defended one another's territory if ever it were threatened. The women with the keeper ruled their families with a rod of iron and won our respect for the consistency of their views and their behaviour. The schoolboy on the left, smartly dressed in his cap and blazer, would not have dreamed of doing anything other than wait his turn. Children knew their place and it was in the queue behind these pillars of society. The zoological gardens had long been a fixture, dating back to when John Jennison acquired the land in 1836. His small zoo grew with more land acquisition until, by Edwardian times, it occupied 69 acres behind its walls with a further 97 acres beyond. By then Belle Vue had become a huge entertainment complex with themed cafés and bars with three entrances being served from four railway stations. The zoo closed in 1967 and a major chapter in the Manchester leisure story came to an end.

Below: The date given for this photograph is 1957, though the costumes worn by people in the crowd at Belle Vue fun fair would appear to be from a decade earlier. The Caterpillar remained a popular ride for many years and was a rather more thrilling experience than the Ocean Wave which was one of Belle Vue's first amusements, and was popular during the 1920s. Tame by today's hair raising standards, the Ocean Wave was built after the 'Sea on Land' type of ride that was common in Victorian times. The bridge of a ship was created on a large roundabout amid scenery that was painted to look like storm dashed waves. As an internal machine rotated the roundabout, small boats set among the waves rose and fell to the accompaniment of squeals of delight from the boats' occupants. Other amusements that were popular during the very early years of Belle Vue was its fledgling zoo. Back then people had little experience of the wider world and its fauna, and six policemen had to control the huge crowds who mobbed the amusement park to see an orang utan billed as the 'Wild Man of Borneo'.

Right: During the 1940s and 50s a fun day out meant a day at Belle Vue, not just for Mancunians but for families across the North of England, and millions went through the turnstiles of the pleasure park when Belle Vue was at its peak of popularity. Many readers will remember the little pleasure steamer 'Little Eastern'; the whole family would enjoy the sail around the large boating lake, and the pleasure of the passengers in the photograph is reflected in their wide smiles. The motor boat was no doubt popular with dads who might otherwise have found themselves expending muscle power with a pair of oars.

would of course have to be applied for and granted by the Corporation. Perhaps four or five times a year competitors would gather in the Park, and 50 or 60 riders would power around the circuit (which was roughly one and a half miles), completing 40 or so laps. Riders Bill Bradley, Geoff Broadbent and Derek Clark often finished as winners and were well known in their day. The photograph was taken in 1950. The riders look quite relaxed, making it more probable that the race is over, the winner declared and it is time to adjourn to the pub to dissect the race. Students' track events were often held in Fallowfield Stadium, Stretford. Reg

Below: Promoted by Len Myatt, who still lives in the area, the 50-mile cycle race was a regular event held in Heaton Park, Manchester. Permission to hold the race Harris, a regular winner, was amateur sprint champion on the 100m track. Harris eventually took over the running of Manchester Athletic Club.

Above: School trips in a chara or double decker bus were difficult to arrange for Wythenshawe pupils in 1948 because fuel and spare cash were both at a premium. Fortunately, the local park was almost as enjoyable for a day out as taking a trip further afield. The teachers packed up crates full of beanbags, skipping ropes, rubber quoits and tennis balls so that relay races could be organised. There were games of leap frog and tunnel ball to be played and some of the lads brought their cricket bats along. Jack and Eric dampened their hair and slicked it back in the style of Denis Compton, the original Brylcreem boy who the summer before had notched up over 3,000 runs for Middlesex. Sheila and Jane made daisy chains and wore them as necklaces as they strutted coquet-

ran merrily through the shadows that dappled the ground under a clear, blue sky on that summer's day half a century ago. Rationing may have meant that the butter on their sandwiches was thinly spread and the meat portions were meagre, but they were free spirits and that was worth all the coupons in their mother's handbag. The young boy enjoying the shade of the tree was a product of the baby boom postwar years when families were reunited after years of enforced separation and nature took its course. The stork put in for time and a half as the birth rate rocketed and Farley's sold out of rusks. Perhaps the girls skipping down the hill were rushing to tell their mother that they had really seen a boggart, that mischievous sprite renowned for playing impish pranks, though more likely the true little imps are held captured forever in the centre of the camera lens.

Above: Slightly reminiscent of a scene from Arthur Ransome's 'Swallows and Amazons' these happy boaters enjoyed the fun of the lake at Heaton Park in 1949. Out on the waters they could imagine that they were sailing off on some adventure or were taking part in a mini University Boat Race. The park is a wonderful place in which to spend the day as there is so much variety and space. When Pope John-Paul II said Mass here in 1982 over 1,000,000 were in the congregation. There are some ten listed buildings to enjoy, including the magnificent Heaton Hall, built in 1777 by James Wyatt for Sir Thomas Egerton. Combined with the pretty orangery, the Hall has become a popular place for wedding ceremonies. Kiddies love the farm centre and being able to see the animals at close quarters and there is plenty of room in the 640 acres of parkland for horticultural gardens, pitch and putt and an 18 hole golf course. Just as they did over 50 years ago families still come to picnic and play large family games of cricket on the grass, just as older generations did before them.

tishly like Rita Hayworth in 'The Lady from Shanghai'. One of the staff lolled against the tree, happily puffing on a Craven A without any fear that he was being a bad influence on his charges. They all enjoyed the break from times tables, spelling tests and handwriting practice as they relaxed in the 250 acres donated in 1926 by Lord and Lady Simon. Wythenshawe Hall, dating from 1540, was one of the park's main features and a former home to the Tatton family. It underwent major alterations in the 19th century and now houses an interesting art collection.

Left: There is a carefree time in our lives that we wish we could bottle and take with us for evermore. When we were young and innocent the world was so simple, just a never ending round of fun and games. Pictured in Boggart Hole Clough in 1951 these swimsuited girls will now be dreaming of bus passes and retirement, but they will spare more than a passing thought for the days when they

Above: At first glance this might appear to be a scene taken from the leafy lanes of Cheshire or some quiet suburban spot on the edge of the countryside, so it may come as a surprise to realise that in 1957 these prams were being pushed in grounds within the closest of Manchester's parks to the city centre. The prams look dated as modern mums now wheel their offspring in sleek multi purpose vehicles that can be converted into pushchairs and car seats. Whitworth Park's 18 acres are situated on Oxford Road and were presented to the council in 1905 by the trustees of the estate of Sir Joseph Whitworth, the celebrated engineer and philanthropist. Born in Stockport in 1803, Whitworth developed a keen interest in the machinery of the industrial revolution and set up a precision engineering company in Chortlton Street in 1833. This was to be the forerunner of his great Whitworth works in Openshaw where he revolutionised accuracy levels from the accepted one sixteenth of an inch to a remarkable one thousandth. The Whitworth screw thread was the norm until metrication in the 1970s. Whitworth Art Gallery, now owned by the University of Manchester, is situated within the park and has a fine collection of wallpapers and textiles in addition to its paintings by Lowry, Hockney and other artists.

The woodland and open green spaces in Wythenshawe Park made for a delightful backdrop to the sandpits and paddling pool where these children splashed around without a care in the world in 1955. They removed their shoes and socks, girls hitched up their skirts and they all rushed happily in and out of the water before racing off for a game of hide and seek amongst the trees. Further over a budding Max Faulkner or Peter Alliss practised his golf swing on the pitch and putt course before joining the rest of the family for potted meat sandwiches and a bottle of Vimto. There were still those who had to keep a tight hold on their purse strings, but better times were just around the corner. The naive joy these children showed when playing on the swings and dipping their toes in the pool is something that parents cherished because a decade earlier they had not been sure if such happiness would touch their lives again.

John Jennison, the founder of Belle Vue Gardens, died in 1869, but his family continued the enterprise that eventually grew to become one of the major leisure attractions in the whole of the country. Rail connections and huge parking lots for cars and charabancs meant that access was excellent. Dance halls, dining suites, concert and sports halls, ice skating rinks, the zoo, speedway, a circus and funfairs were just some of the facilities that must have attracted millions of visitors through the turnstiles in the 20th century in the sure knowledge that they were guaranteed a great day out. Belle Vue enjoyed a huge boom after World War II as the nation demanded a lift for their lives in the austere recovery days of the 1950s. The Bobs and the Caterpillar were amongst the best patronised of the many attractions in the funfair. 'Bobbing' up and down on a roller coaster ride as girls screamed with a mixture of joy and fright may seem tame to modern youth, but in 1957 it was one of the scariest sensations around. For a quieter moment couples could cuddle under the Caterpillar canopy, safe in the knowledge that mum could not see what they were up to. She had a good idea, though, because she had taken that same ride with dad 20 years earlier.

Above: Manchester's Opera House is one of the best known theatres outside the West End, often putting on major productions by prestigious companies. In 1968 it was the turn of the Festival Ballet Company to delight us with its performance of Tchaikovsky's 'Sleeping Beauty', one of the most wonderful of ballets that has been graced by all the greats from Nijinsky to Nureyev and Pavlova to Fonteyn. The original intent for the Opera House, or New Theatre as it began life in 1912, was to provide Manchester with a new Shakespearean theatre and centre for grand opera. Designed by Farquharson, Richardson and Gill and holding 3,000 people paying from sixpence to five shillings, the Quay Street building was to undergo several changes of name in quick succession. In 1915 it became the New Queen's Theatre and two years later the New Queen's Theatre and Opera House, before settling on its present title in 1920. In the 1940s and 1950s the audiences packed in to see such musical extravaganzas as 'Oklahoma', 'The King and I' and 'West Side Story'. Theatre going declined in the following two decades to the degree that the Opera House closed in 1979, briefly becoming a Mecca bingo hall. Thankfully it was restored to its true place in entertainment when it reopened under the Palace Theatre's ownership in 1984.

Top: By 1967 the Rialto on Bury New Road, Higher Broughton had become part of the ABC network of cinemas. The film 'Zulu', starring Michael Caine and Stanley Baker, had taken its time to arrive as it had been filmed in 1964. The adjacent buildings housed the Riverboat Club and Whisky a Gogo, illustrating the changing fashions in entertainment that in the late 60s and 70s spawned a mixture of establishments offering dance music and live acts. As time went on Wythenshawe's Golden Garter, Chorlton's Princess Club, North Manchester's Embassy and similar venues played host to the revival tours of acts whose stars had waned. They also provided openings for comics to make a name for themselves and a number progressed to national fame for a while via television's 'The Comedians'. Mike Burton, Ken Goodwin, Duggie Brown, Charlie Williams and George Roper were just some of the men for whom stardom came after years on the northern club circuit. 'The Wheeltappers and Shunters' Club', an amusing parody on working men's clubs, was also popular on the box.

Above: Comedian Tommy Cooper and constable Edward McLernon of Manchester and Salford Police are supported by a 'backing group' of pupils of Rack House Junior School, Wythenshawe, Manchester, as they sing Partridge Green's "Green Cross Code" song to PC McLernon traditional folk melody. The song was recorded by singer Partridge Green and copies of the record and the sheet music were supplied to all schools in Manchester and Salford, for use in teaching the Green Cross Code. It was launched in the early 1970s to train young children to cross the road in safety.

Facing page and right: George Best, Manchester United's young mop-topped winger, doesn't confine his genius to the football field, gives the final set to one of his creations before a fashion show at Tiffany's, a Manchester night club, on 30 September 1966. Earlier in the year, after United's 5-1 victory over Benfica in the quarter finals of the European Cup, Best was proclaimed by one Portuguese newspaper as "El Beatle". Inevitably when back at home he would be dubbed the 'fifth Beatle'. Together with his close friend Mike Summerbee, of Manchester City, George Best opened a number of fashion boutiques in Manchester, which were run by Malcolm Mooney. He ended up having a stake in three shops, as well as 'Edwardia' in Sale he also had a shop just off Deansgate and a third in the Arndale Shopping precinct. Best also ventured into the travel agency business and opened a couple of nightclubs, Slack Alice's and Oscars.

Belle Vue Lake and Firework Island, pictured here in 1949. Spectacular annual firework displays were held at Belle Vue for many years. This took the form of a play with actors, usually featuring a battle of some kind or perhaps having a piratical theme. Whatever the theme the audience could always expect lots of thrilling bangs, crashes and flashes. The 1926 show was 'The Reign of Terror'; in 1936 the ballet 'San Sebastian 1836' was staged. Firework displays, discontinued during World War II, were reintroduced in 1947, though without actors. In 1954 a move was made to reintroduce the old battlepieces, and 'The Storming of Quebec' was staged.

The show, which had synchronised sound tracks and 250 actors, took many months of rehearsal to bring it to perfection, and the actual performances lasted for thirty minutes. The show was planned to last for eight weeks but in the end had to be extended in response to popular demand. 'The Relief of Lucknow' was performed in 1955 and 'Robin Hood' the following year. But audiences were falling as the public demanded more sophisticated effects. After the 1956 performance only ordinary firework displays were put on, and even these were discontinued in 1969.

THOSE WERE THE DAYS!

Each generation thinks of itself as modern at every stage of life and yet we are all relics and mementoes of our own history. As time goes by, we try to hang on to our more modish and fashionable behaviour and attitudes, sometimes with the thought that we can defy the passing of time with our constant recreation of 'the past'. Even so, most people enjoy looking back and remembering with affection things done or achieved and comparing the context of their early lives with improvements sometimes made in more recent times. Things often seem not to be as good as in the 'olden days', but most of the time we are not looking at a level playing field. Inevitably, many of our childhood memories, whatever our age now, are of endless summers and snow-filled winters, a sort of historically appropriate version of Dylan Thomas's 'A Child's Christmas in Wales'. But, for all of us, time marches on and, as we get older, it seems strange that we find ourselves attempting to explain to a nine year old god-daughter that there was life of a sort before computers, emphasising simultaneously our incredibly ancient origins! Wartime experiences and memories often define

generations, although with involvement in more recent conflicts, even this timeline has had to be redefined. The progress in radio and TV development has outstripped most people's imagination and provided a sometimes obsessive and questionable way of filling our days. Until the middle of the 20th century, children often had to use their own imagination, inventiveness and creativity. The streets were filled with groups of children of different ages pretending to be somebody, somewhere and something else. This was fun for most, freeing and gentle in its stimulation, and engendered a relevant and satisfactory competitiveness conducive to learning.

This page: Outdoors including in the playground, improvisation was the name of the game. You didn't need a ball for football - a tightly bound bundle of rags or clothes would do. There were games that matched the seasons, conkers for example. Those determined to win used foul and dishonest ways to convert the simple conker into a hard and unyielding boulder to cheat their way to success. Later in the year it was marbles with those wonderful glass beads put to aggressive and

and Charlie Shaw, with Bob Hodgkinson seated. The names of the children are unknown.

Below centre: In the 1950s, toys were still quite simple, for boys and girls. In a society that continued to place the emphasis on women as home makers and child producers, toymakers were still making a lot of money from selling pretty little dolls to pretty little girls, banking on their softness for small, defenceless creatures in their own image. This wonderful picture, taken in 1950, shows two such little girls enjoying posing for a 'family' photograph, repeated no doubt twenty years later as the real thing. Note the grittily determined, no-nonsense expression of the young lady at the back and the rather shyer, slightly myopic expression of the seated young lady with hair that, possibly, she has spent the rest of her life not being able to 'do a thing with'!

Below: The influence of Errol Flynn in the 1940s is obvious here in a game involving bows and arrows. His playing of Robin Hood against Olivia de Havilland as Maid Marian had a ground-breaking impact for some little boys that remained with them to their teenage years (and in some cases even longer!). Cinema has always had an influence on children's re-enactment and performance of stories and fables. Certainly children in the 1940s rarely complained about boredom or having nothing to do. They simply grasped the nettle and worked out what they could turn it into and did it together.

destructive use to determine who was top dog. There were also collecting activities, usually involving cards with familiar faces, often of footballers or film stars. Playground games were often determined by gender, with the differences usually marked by the polarising of physical prowess and single-mindedness on the one hand and a softer camaraderie and togetherness on the other. All the equipment and artefacts used in play were simple, often loud and often extremely irritating in their use and application, but great fun!

Above: Many Bethel Chapels follow the mission statement, 'to turn the lost into the found and the faithless into the faithful'. The word 'Bethel' is taken from two Hebrew words, 'bêt' and 'el', meaning the house of God. 'Chapel' is derived from the Latin 'cappella', meaning cloak. The building, therefore, provided a secret place where dissenters could worship God. Chapels were originally breakaway places, shattering the mould by providing a place of worship for those who objected to the status quo. In the dark days of the 1920s, poverty was rife. Many poor families had little in the way of either hope or sustenance. They simply got poorer. This soup kitchen at Bethel Chapel offered a form of gruel and bread to the needy. The people in the picture are, from left to right, EE Bell, Harry Barnet, Mr Blakely

Right: The group of unknown kiddies, pictured here in the late 19th century, were the lucky ones. Dressed up in their finery, including the borrowing of a few fathers' flat caps, they looked the picture of health. In all probability, they would live to a ripe old age. Some of their siblings were not so fortunate. Insanitary living conditions for the working classes, poor diets and no such things as antibiotics, penicillin or mass immunisation meant that youngsters fell prey to a host of childhood diseases. Scarlet fever, whooping cough and measles, to name but a few.

was brought inside on a Saturday night, whether you needed an all over scrub or not. Waiting in front of a roaring fire, with kettles of boiling water being prepared, was part of the routine. This little lass obviously had her own individual model. Young Doreen or Dorothy, whatever her name was, could make the fun of bathtime last right up to the final 'Come on young lady, beddie-byes' was repeated in an exasperated voice.

Above: Little pedal cars were all the rage, especially for young boys, in the 1930s. Motoring was booming and toy manufacturers spotted the opportunity of a new niche in the market. While less affluent parents bought their children scooters for Christmas, Santa Claus packed his sleigh with imitations of real motorcars for the offspring of the wealthy. Some cars actually featured windows that really moved, working horns and lights, real chrome, bonnet ornaments, white wall tyres and custom paint. Many of the cars were made from metal, though this became less likely in the 1940s as the war effort demanded that such materials were channelled into the manufacture of military ordnance.

Right: Even in the middle of the last century, not all homes had bathrooms. Some of the older properties relied on outside toilets and the tin bath in the yard that

Below: Conditions may have been grim on occasions but there was usually time for a warm smile and friendly chat in the street. These were the days when people routinely left their doors unlocked or open, without fear of someone running off with their television. Of course, they didn't have a television, but you know what we mean! These days the neighbourly culture which we used to take for granted has disappeared from many areas and some people seem to know the characters in the popular soap operas better than the people next door. It would be unusual, to say the least, to see a modern housewife scrubbing the pavement outside her house in this day and age.

appliances or white goods to make the task of running the house any easier. Many families lived in terraced housing, some of it back to back, with outdoor lavvies, where you learned to whistle

with one foot against the door in case someone else attempted to enter this little smelly enclave of privacy. Many houses still had a tin bath that was dragged in from the yard and filled with kettle after kettle of boiling water before family members took it in turn to soak themselves. This photograph, dating from the 1950s, shows a typical scene from life at the time; families and communities were close knit, sharing each other's joys and sorrows. It was quite common to lend a neighbour a helping hand in times of need and this was often more than just a cup of sugar. Friendships were formed that lasted a lifetime.

Top right and right: At one time, Monday was the traditional washday for many. For working class families, the burden fell upon mum. Her role as a housewife meant that the day was spent boiling clothes in a tub and wringing them out through the mangle before pegging out on the line in a back yard, or similar. Before the days of sophisticated washing powders and rubber gloves, reddened hands were her reward and yet there were still beds to be made, carpets to beat and lino to wash. The children needed feeding and the evening meal had to be ready when dad got home. It was hard work and there were few, if any, modern electrical

This page: It was the Victorians who helped popularise the beach holiday when steam trains opened up the coastline for mill and factory workers to take their annual leave at Scarborough or Blackpool. Until then, such resorts were either out of reach or lay undeveloped. By the early 20th century, the seaside was a good place to indulge in a little naughtiness as young men showed off their muscles and young ladies displayed flesh that was normally hidden away under tightly laced corsets and voluminous skirts. The two cuties under the parasol look to be taking a particular coquettish delight in baring that which their mums never dared do outside the bedroom. Even then, the lights had to be off. The pair of young men often fancied themselves as the sort to get the girls' pulse racing. Let us face it, which red blooded female would not be driven wild with frenzy at the sight of those knees or the manly pose of the one with hands on hips, suggesting he was up for it, as they say today?

The lady posing alone, though very fetching, failed to catch the attention of the deck chair attendant. A true northerner, he wanted cash first and voyeurism later.

Facing page, centre: On the beach, on those odd days that the sun shone, we largely made up our own entertainment. There were the traditional donkey rides and Punch and Judy shows that we paid to enjoy, but the rest of the time was spent in amusing ourselves. Apart from the obvious splashing about and swimming in the sea, every family had a cricket bat, tennis ball and set of stumps. Miniature Ashes Tests were played. Ornate sand castles were created and dad was the long suffering sort who did not mind too much being buried in the sand, yet again. Mini Olympics were organised with obstacle races, three legged events, leap frog games and stone skimming tourneys. Youngsters wandered off to explore rock pools and fill little buckets with crabs and other sea creatures. Adventurous kiddies disappeared for hours, but we knew that they would be safe.

Right: Who cared if the sun shone or the heavens opened? We had come to the seaside, paid our tanner for the deckchair and claimed our spot on the beach. Here we were going to stay for the rest of the day, hail, rain or shine. Our only acknowledgement that the weather would have any effect upon us was if we had to put on a raincoat or turn up a collar if the wind blew too hard. For the best part of the year, our fingers had been worked to the bone slaving over looms and shuttles or hewing coal from seams deep underground. When the annual holiday week, or fortnight if you were very lucky, came around, families packed their

seen active service in the desert sands of North Africa, but it was to the beaches of Lancashire that they returned for their recreation each summer. Of course, anyone could go and paddle in the sea, but it had not always been so. There was a time when certain stretches of coast were reserved at particular times of the year. In 1900, a railway poster stated that sea bathing time at parts of Fleetwood and Blackpool had been set aside for the working classes on several weekends.

buckets and spades and made for the seaside, often finding their way to the same guest house that they had used the year before, and the year before that as well. Even if the landlady was a bit on the forbidding side, with her rules and regulations and 6.30 sharp message for the evening meal, it was the consistency that was liked.

Right: The family group posing in 1947 with Blackpool Tower as a backdrop had been here many times over the years. The place acted like a magnet for holidaymakers. The menfolk may have

Above: When the baby boomer generation went to school in the early 1950s, it had benefited from the 1944 Education Act that brought free education to all primary and secondary aged children. For the first time, there was a level playing field, to use a school based analogy. Of course, that field had its bumps and muddy portions because perfection and complete equality could not be guaranteed. Those going to school in leafy suburbs tended to do better than those where slag heaps overlooked the grimy villages. But, at least working class kids had the chance of better and further education. Such lofty thoughts were not in the minds of youngsters enjoying the playground. The lad in the background obviously fancied himself as Roy Rogers or Tom Mix as he played on the rocking horse and checked behind him that pesky injuns were not on his trail. The girls, of course, enjoyed dressing the dolls as another couple had fun on the see-saw. They did not bump it too hard as the lads did when they had their turn.

Right: This very 'typical' photograph, taken in 1960, reminds many of us how much we looked forward to that afternoon period which included 'games', particularly in the summer, the sound of willow on leather (not always!), the chance to compete and play in a team; the chap on the right doesn't look too pleased - maybe that's because he's carrying the rounders bat and is already worrying that he might have to play with the girls - NO WAY! - and it was ever so. From the well-developed greenery behind and the wearing of woolly tops one must surmise that we are looking at a late summer scene with the chance to impress and become part of the school team long gone. On the left of the picture the games teacher in her whites suggests it's summer and she will still demand 100% effort from

everybody; after an initial scramble on the field to find a place on the boundary - less stressful, less running - provided you could throw, we all accepted our lot and relaxed the afternoon away, just glad, for once, to be out of the classroom

Above: Out of necessity, road safety has become a major issue for all of us in our lifetimes and has been written into the school curriculum since the middle of the 20th century. As we can see in photographs from earlier in the last century that appear in this book, children played games in the streets and rode their bicycles on the carriageway with little danger to life or limb. With the steadily increasing traffic in the 1930s, safety became an obvious and challenging issue and, with accident statistics rising alarmingly, the government of the day was obliged to take action. Driving tests were introduced, Belisha Beacon crossings appeared in towns and cities and that well-known bestseller, The Highway Code, was formulated and published. In this photograph taken in 1950, youngsters are given instruction on a model roadway system. Stop, look and listen were watchwords drummed into children together with instruction on how to signal correctly and how to use crossings safely. In later years, we saw the Tufty Club, the Green Cross Code and, frighteningly, a fully permed Kevin Keegan advising us on why it was NOT a good idea to run out from behind parked cars! Sometimes, it all seemed a little light-hearted, but at least it got the point over.

Right: When Ernest Evans asked whether it was a bird or a plane up there and answered himself by telling us that it was a twister, a craze was born that swept dance floors across the western world. He also made sure that countless numbers of children would be

embarrassed at weddings, 21st dos and parties during the 1990s as their parents risked hernias and heart attacks attempting to twist the night away whilst their offspring raised their eyes to heaven. Evans was a fan of the 1950s rocker Fats Domino and used his name as the inspiration for becoming known as Chubby Checker. Oddly, his first big hit in Britain was in 1963 with 'Let's Twist Again', a follow up to 'The Twist', a record that only became very popular the following year. By 1963, when this couple attempted to keep their seams straight as they gyrated in the front room to the music from their Dansette record player,

SPORTING LIFE

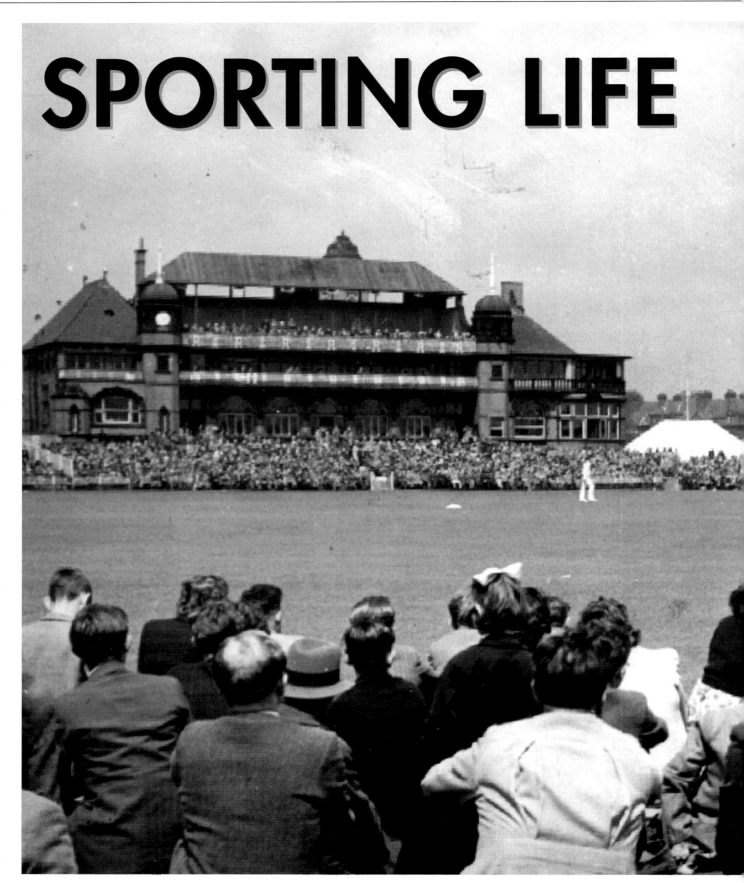

The sound of willow on leather under a balmy, blue sky brought crowds in their thousands to Old Trafford after the second world war. Starved of top class professional sport for so many years the public filled soccer grounds, speedway stadiums and cricket arenas week after week. This game in 1950 had seen people queuing down Talbot Road long before the umpires rang the warning bell that they were about to take to the field. The seats were filled and spectators spilled onto the grass inside the boundary ropes, craning their necks to get a glimpse of Cyril Washbrook and Winston Place about to set off on another opening partnership. It was the start of a fine decade of county championship cricket for Lancashire and it had some fine players who graced the scene. Geoff Edrich, one of a dynasty of excellent batsmen, was a cultured strokemaker and his efforts were well supported by Jack Ikin and the gritty Ken Grieves, whose slip catching ability was helped by his winter employment as a professional goalkeeper. Bob Berry, Roy Tattersall and Malcolm Hilton provided the slow bowling, but it was the speed and accuracy of quickie Brian Statham that wreaked the greatest havoc. Despite all these top players Lancashire could never quite match Surrey, the dominant force in the 1950s that won seven championships.

Below: Manchester speedway racing originally took place at the Greyhound Stadium, but as the sport gained in popularity it was clear that it would need a purpose built stadium. The Belle Vue speedway stadium was opened in March 1929, eight years before this photograph was taken in August of 1937. Originally termed 'dirt track racing', speedway originated in Australia. E O Spence was speedway manager at Belle Vue until 1941. Early in World War II he moved on to become Managing Director of the Belle Vue Company until he died in 1947. Speedway was interrupted by the war for a while, then continued, and the highly successful home team, The Aces, owed much to the skill of riders such as Eric Langton and Frank (Red Devil) Varey. A popular innovation was added to the meetings during 1954 in the form of 'Johnnie's Marching Girls', a British version of the American cheerleader squad. Thirteen young and pretty girls clad in red and white costumes would enliven each speedway meeting with performances at regular intervals. The speedway stadium was often put to alternative uses. Tattoos were held there soon after the stadium was completed, and the spectacular Lancashire Cotton Pageant was staged there in 1932.

Right: The stadium at Belle Vue was opened on 23 March 1929, and was a mecca for devotees of speedway in general and the Aces in particular. Purpose built for the sport, the stadium nevertheless lent itself to a variety of other uses. Stock car racing was introduced in June 1954 with considerable success. Nine meetings were held every year until Belle Vue Stadium closed down. The last stock car event was held on 14th November 1987, and the stadium was demolished only weeks later to make way for a British Car Auction Group development.

Belle Vue's popularity as an all round family entertainment soared during the post war years. But even as early as 1951 attendances were beginning to slip, and only four years later the management were in real trouble. Sir Leslie Joseph and Charles Forte stepped in with a rescue package and transformed the pleasure grounds, giving Belle Vue the new lease of life it so badly needed. Entrances were remodelled, a lot of refurbishments were done, and a large Bingo club was opened in Kings Hall, which proved to be very popular. By 1962 attendances were up again once more.

Supporting Manchester City has always been something of a roller coaster ride, at one time hitting the dizzy heights and on others plummeting to earth in despair. Despite those ups and downs the club has retained a faithful local level of support that is the envy of many others. This 1955 match at Maine Road against Arsenal came during one of those periods of success when City could rightly claim to be on a par with their arch enemies from Old Trafford. That year Wembley beckoned and the team's defeat by Newcastle in the FA Cup Final was heavily influenced by a nasty injury to fullback Jimmy Meadows, reducing the side to ten men in those days when substitutes were not allowed. True to their promise, the players returned to the twin towers 12 months later to defeat Birmingham in a match made even more memorable by another example of the Wembley injury hoodoo. City's keeper, the German Bert Trautmann, broke his neck during the game, but bravely played on. He did not realise how badly he was hurt until after the final whistle. The 1950s were wonderful times for soccer supporters who could enjoy cheering on their teams and swapping banter with visiting supporters. Joe Hayes, Billy Spurdle, Bill Leivers and Roy Paul were the stuff that soccer was made of.

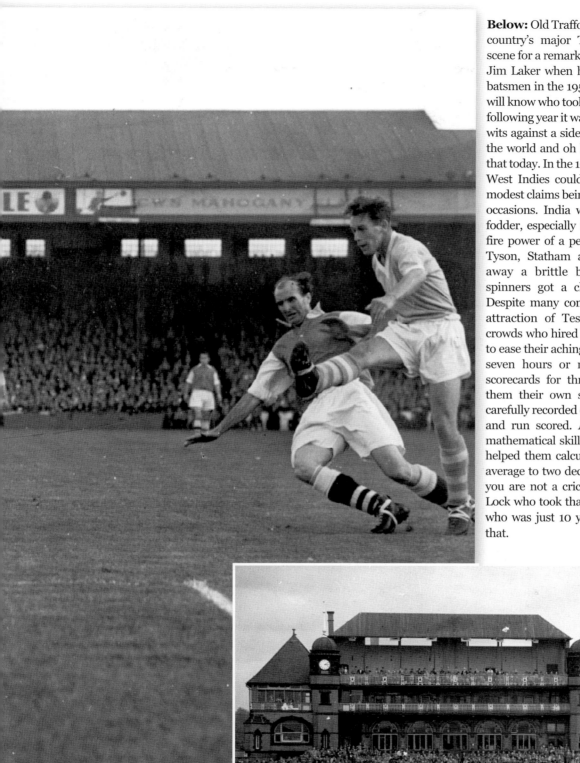

Below: Old Trafford has long been one of the country's major Test centres and was the scene for a remarkable feat of spin bowling by Jim Laker when he dismissed 19 Australian batsmen in the 1956 Ashes match. Quiz buffs will know who took the only other wicket. The following year it was the turn of India to pit its wits against a side that was about the best in the world and oh how we wish we could say that today. In the 1950s only Australia and the West Indies could run us close, with some modest claims being made by South Africa on occasions. India was only so much cannon fodder, especially in English conditions. The fire power of a permutation from Trueman, Tyson, Statham and Loader often blasted away a brittle batting order before the spinners got a chance to have their say. Despite many contests being one sided the attraction of Test cricket brought in the crowds who hired little cushions for a tanner to ease their aching bottoms for a vigil lasting seven hours or more. Schoolboys bought scorecards for threepence or brought with them their own scorebooks in which they carefully recorded every dot ball, wicket taken and run scored. At the end of an innings mathematical skills learned in the classroom helped them calculate each player's bowling average to two decimal places. By the way, if you are not a cricket buff then it was Tony Lock who took that other wicket, but anyone who was just 10 years old back then knows that.

Below: A tense moment in the game between Manchester United FC and Tottenham in 1951 as Jack Rowley runs in to take the ball. Note the thousands upon thousands of fans overflowing the terraces in this dramatic photograph, taken before the rise in popularity of TV sets. Today the ground seats 55,000, but scenes such as this are not seen so often today. TV coverage affected attendance, and while the atmosphere of the game is lost, many still opt to watch the match in the comfort of their own homes with a few cans of the right stuff. United moved to Old Trafford in 1910, and a crowd of 45,000 watched the club play their first match against Liverpool. The Second World War proved a difficult time for Man United; soon after war was declared the game was suspended, and Old Trafford was bombed twice in the space of a few months. In the first season of play after the war, new manager Matt Busby began creating history with his 'Busby Babes'. On his death in 1994, thousands of fans left scarves as a tribute to the great man; the bales of scarves were sealed inside a hollow bronze statue of Sir Matt Busby.

Right: September 1959, and hundreds of United fans crowd the turnstiles. 1959 was a memorable year; the club was still reeling from the effects of the Munich air disaster that took the lives of seven of the 'Busby Babes' on 6th February 1958 and left Matt Busby in a critical condition. Chairman Harold Hardman gave his promise that the club would go on. Many regarded it as an impossible task, as the Babes had featured some of the best players of their generation, but Assistant Manager Jimmy Murphy determinedly set about rebuilding the team. He promoted junior and reserve team players and made emergency signings and the team completed that season's fixtures. The United that emerged possessed its own unique flavour. Wilf McGuinness, Warren Bradley and Albert Quixall came into the side and a 3-1 win over Leicester City secured the FA Cup in the 62/63 season. But the best was yet to be; Bobby Charlton captained United to European Cup victory in May 1968, a thrilling 4-1 win over Benifica at Wembley making United the first English club to win the European Cup. That same year Matt Busby's services to football were acknowledged when he received a knighthood from the Queen.

Above: The grunt and grapple merchants at Belle Vue's King's Hall were a hugely popular attraction that packed the venue for over 25 years after the war. It was far removed from the modern American WWF style of ridiculously staged violence, mayhem and 'in your face' posturing. British professional wrestling was a mixture of skill and humour that crowds appreciated in equal measure. We all knew that most of the fights were rigged, but they were done with such panache that it was almost an art form. Whilst it was true that some little old ladies got carried away and rushed the ring trying to thump some protagonist with an umbrella, most of us sat back and joined in the fun by cheering the good guy and booing the villain. It was

something like a pantomime performed on canvas. There were great families of wrestlers like Harry, Jackie and Bully Pye, refereed with increasing frustration by such as Dick the Dormouse. There were characters a-plenty with Masambula, the Simba Kid and Bert Royal. Who ever would have thought that Big Daddy was really Shirley Crabtree and that he lived in a little rural village in West Yorkshire? However, some of us guessed that Kurt Nielsen, despite his Viking helmet, actually turned a lathe by day at Mitchell and Shackleton in Patricroft and that his real name was much more mundane. The wrestling at King's Hall could always be guaranteed to finish at 10 pm so that the audience could get to the local in time for last orders. If the final bout began at 9.55 you knew a first round knockout was a certainty.

Below: Kings Hall, Belle Vue, was a focal point for wrestling and boxing enthusiasts. Though the sport was discontinued for the duration of World War II, it quickly re-established its reputation during the post war years. This atmospheric photograph, which dates from around 1960, gives us a taste of what it must have been like in its heyday, when vast crowds converged upon the hall, rooting for well known wrestlers such as Jack Pye, who emerged as one of Belle Vue's major sporting personalities between the 1940s

and 1960s. Surprisingly for the time before women's lib had burnt many of its bras, the promotion of wrestling at Belle Vue was undertaken by Kathleen Look. Miss Look was Britain's only woman promoter; her highly professional handling of the job brought credit to the sport. Kings Hall, one of the largest outside London, was the venue for many types of event. An annual Christmas Circus was staged there (though the ceiling was too low for high wire acts). During the 1960s it became the largest Bingo hall in the country, and the popular game was played at Kings Hall twice every week. Audiences rioted, however, during a Rolling Stones concert on 8th August 1964.

Right: Heaton Park is the largest municipal park in Europe. The former estate of the Earls of Wilton has been owned by Manchester City Council since 1902 and represents 25 per cent of the green space in Manchester. In this 1948 still shot the mill chimneys in the distance remind us of the cotton trade that was so important to Lancashire, but was about to go into terminal decline. They were also partly responsible for the continual haze that hung over the city, turning to choking smog in the late autumn and winter months. People clutched hankies to the mouths or made little masks out of strips of material held on by pieces of elastic. The various

Clean Air Acts of the 1950s helped improve the environment to a degree we had never imagined possible. These men's shirts were grimy with specks of soot and dirt that hung around in the atmosphere. They took that for granted as they carefully balanced the virtues of thumb or finger bias, sending their woods skidding across the turf in a geometric

arc. The 2002 Commonwealth Games used Heaton Park's four greens for its bowls competition and the standard was a far cry from old man's marbles as youngsters once dubbed the game. The park is listed as Grade II on English Heritage's register of historic parks and gardens.

AROUND THE SHOPS

Top: Paulden's, at the top of Market Street as it enters Piccadilly, became Debenham's, but it had flourished long before then on Stretford Road. This shot of the mighty department store was taken in 1925, by which time it had been established for nearly 50 years, and the company went on to give the city a century of service. Those of us who were brought up in and around Manchester will have their own fond memories of shopping here. We also remember the tricks that our mothers got up to. Five or six weeks before the Whit Friday Walks, known as Scholars' Walks, mums would head off on the bus on a journey of espionage. They carefully scrutinised and mentally recorded the patterns of the new season's dresses exhibited in Paulden's display windows and, using practised skills, ran up close copies and cut down versions for their daughters to wear in the Whit procession. When it came time for a new school uniform mum continued to show that typical Mancunian blend of thrift and nous. Henry Barrie's in St. Anne's Square was the official supplier of school uniforms but this monopoly meant that the clothing was pricey. You had to have the official tie, but it made more sense to buy a badge from Barrie's and sew it onto the right colour of blazer bought at Paulden's, Lewis's or Affleck and Brown for half the price.

Above right: It seems to be something of a waste of resources to have a policeman on point duty when all that can be seen for him to direct amounts to one horse and cart and a bicycle far off in the distance. On 7 June 1940 people had left their cars at home, restricted as they were to a few

miles of personal motoring each week. They went back to forms of transport that had served them well before the days of the internal combustion engine and that included using Shanks's pony as the woman on the right was doing. This generation thought nothing of walking miles and would be horrified to see 21st century mums in 4x4 cars and people carriers driving their children 200 yards to school. The building behind the bobby had contained a swimming pool, as can be determined from the lettering and the raised relief of a diver on the facade of the top storey. Manchester's archives record this photograph as showing the junction with Bridge Street, but there are arguments to place the scene further down the road at Quay Street. Whatever the location there was a job for the constable to perform, but as it was quiet he could have been forgiven for letting his mind wander as he recalled Churchill's stirring words, 'We shall defend our island whatever the cost may be,' uttered three days before.

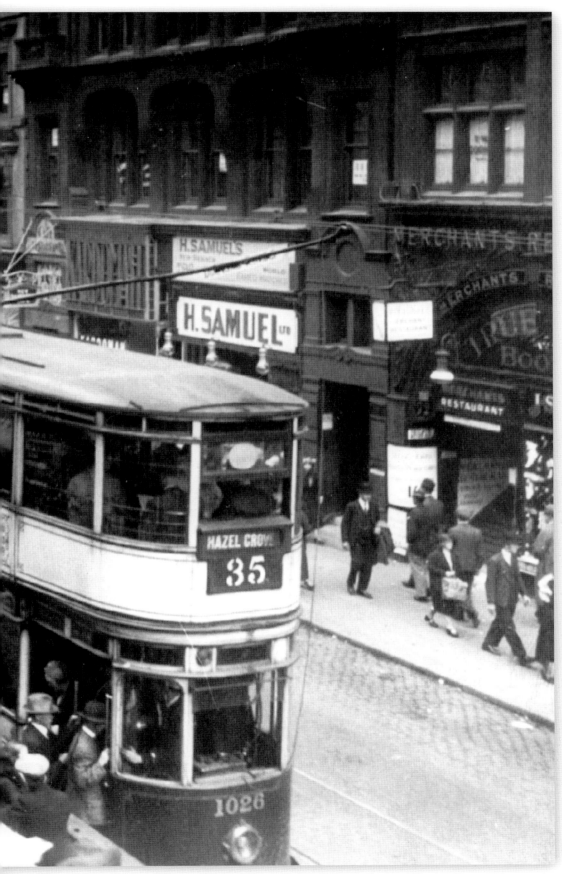

Market Street adopted its present name in the early 1800s and by 1939 had long been established as one of the main shopping areas of the city. Here we are looking towards Piccadilly with Lewis's on the right, a famous name that disappeared only in recent years. That department store was a favourite meeting place on a Saturday night for lovers who had travelled separately into Manchester and disembarked from their transport at the nearby bus station. Unfortunately, there were one or two ladies of dubious reputation who used to frequent the area, but the police kept a careful eye on them and usually moved them into Tib Street to book them as it was easier to spell than Piccadilly. The horse and cart at the bottom of the photograph remind us of the bygone age when rag and bone men came round the streets offering a donkey stone for the front step in exchange for whatever odds and ends we wished to throw out. The noble horse was once seen in great numbers on Manchester's streets, helping to provide public transport. The forerunner to this Hazel Grove tram, the horse drawn variety, operated until the end of Victoria's reign. Manchester Carriage Company, formed in 1865, eventually owned 385 trams and 3,583 horses. As each animal produced four tons of manure each year it was good news for rhubarb and roses.

Below: Looking along Market Street in 1957 the no waiting signs were the first attempts made to relieve congestion along this favourite shopping area. It is now pedestrianised and some of its shops now suffer from the fast food syndrome as the previous tenants moved into the Arndale Centre or on elsewhere. The man walking towards Preston's jewellers passed another looking into the window at Direct Raincoat, an establishment that promised it could undercut some of the bigger tailoring names. By the time the 1960s came along many traditional outfitters found it difficult to survive as jeans and T-shirts became the fashion and bright boutiques clamoured for the custom of that new consumer force, the teenager. Timpson's shoes had to battle hard for business against Tru-form, Saxone and Dolcis in a cut-throat business world. In 1957 it was stiletto heels on which young women tottered, much to the concern of the medical profession who felt that their feet would be deformed. Dance hall owners were not too thrilled either when they found pockmarked floors after an evening session. Young men also tested the doctors' nerves with their choice of footwear. Winklepickers with tapering tips cramped the feet quite painfully, but the lads about town did not care as they were the perfect complement to their luminous socks.

Right: Hope Brothers and Horne's are in this photograph, but the building on the right takes the eye. Marks and Spencer has moved around the Market Street area over the years, partly because of economic restructuring but also of necessity after the IRA bombing of 1996. In 1955 it was attracting its usual large share of custom to the store that opened in November 1931. Its original area of 18,000 square feet would be extended as business grew and the name became synonymous with quality and keen pricing. The company dominated the middle ground, particularly in the clothing trade, but its reputation became tarnished in the 1990s when accusations of drabness and fuddy-duddy styling were levelled at its products. However, the business seemed to have turned the corner and was attracting plaudits once more early into the new millennium. Michael Marks, 'don't ask the price it's a penny', began running bazaars before joining forces with Thomas Spencer in 1894. By the 1930s Marks and Sparks, as it affectionately became known, was established on many town centre streets. It can even argue that St Michael is the patron saint of underwear. Rows of skirts, jumpers and blouses sit alongside the children's wear. Many is the time you have been kitted out for the new school year in a Marks & Spencer grey shirt, blue jersey and pleated skirt or trousers if you were a boy.

A few unsure pedestrians hesitate as they cross Market Street in 1938. There are no traffic lights at the junction of Market Street and Corporation Street at this time, though they were added in later years as can be seen on the following page. With the benefit of hindsight and the ability to compare old photographs we can note the changes that would be made at this spot in future years. The large corner shop on the left was Stones electrical stores, and the board mounted on top of the building advertises their radios. By the 1950s the board had disappeared and the store had become Beaty's. Prosser's pawn shop next door survived the years intact, however, until the redevelopment of 1958 cut a swathe through this area of the city. The road was still cobbled when this photograph was taken, and tram lines still in place. Manchester's trams rattled through the city streets until 1949. The car in the centre which is about to head off across the junction is a 1938 model Hillman Minx. The company were fortunate in securing a contract to carry on producing the model for government use throughout World War II.

Above: A solitary car waits at the traffic lights at the junction of Market Street, Corporation Street and Cross Street, and the block of shops and offices opposite wears a tired and desolate air. The signs above the shops tell us the reason, and forty years on the wording of the notices still conveys the anger and resentment of the traders in the area that was earmarked for redevelopment. 'Forced out after 50 years' the pawnbroker Prosser & Son's sign tells us bitterly, while Beaty Brothers on the corner spells it out for us: 'Premises to be Demolished'. The desperate protests had no effect however on those who had already decreed otherwise, and within months these old buildings that had served the city well had vanished for ever. Before long the thirty acre site would lose its pubs, shops, banks, hotels and shops and would bristle with tower cranes and scaffolding. A landscaped pedestrian area eventually emerged from the organised chaos to be appreciated by the next generation of shoppers who had never known Market Street as it was in this photograph. Just off picture to the right is the Royal Exchange, which was the centre of Manchester's commercial life for many years.

Bottom left: Many readers will no doubt have fond memories of the Alhambra Cinema in Ashton Old Road, Openshaw. The Alhambra ended up as a typical suburban cinema. Nevertheless the building has an interesting history. Built in 1910 as a theatre, the Alhambra for some time entertained local residents with its popular music hall turns. As the 'talkies' began to gain popularity the management very wisely forestalled the possible defection of their audiences to 'picture houses' by converting the theatre to a dual purpose attraction. The rear of the building became the Pavilion, where films were shown, while the Alhambra continued as a theatre. Alhambra audiences declined, however, and in 1916 the Alhambra became a cinema while the Pavilion was turned into a dance hall! A confusing but understandable move by an obviously enterprising management. In an area of mixed residential, shopping and industrial use that had a number of other cinemas, the entertainment offered by the Alhambra had to meet the demands of the customer. The Alhambra survived until 1960.

Below: Market Street, traditionally one of the busiest spots in the city, has seen many dramatic changes since this photograph was taken in 1957. A No 77 Reddish bus - probably a Stockport Corporation vehicle - waits for the traffic lights to change (note the lack of advertising on the side), while a lovely old car is sandwiched between the newer A30 and the cream Ford. Henry's was the shop on the left with the ornate canopy, and Hope Brothers outfitters had the large corner site. Market Street was always a popular place to shop, made accessible by the nearby Piccadilly Station and the availability of the multitude of trams and buses that passed up and down the street. Manchester's massive redevelopment of the Market Street area in the 1970s added the pedestrianised area, undercover shopping and the Arndale Centre, rendering the street unrecognisable to former Mancunians revisiting the city after a number of years' absence. It was this development, of course, that twenty years later took the force of the massive IRA bomb that devastated the heart of the city on 15 June 1996. 80,000 shoppers and workers were evacuated in time to avoid fatalities, though 200 people were injured.

Alexandra Road runs south of the city, parallel to Princess Road, through Moss Side, the district that officially became part of Manchester in 1904. By 1960, when this warmly clad shopper was examining the hardware on the pavement, the population of the area had changed during the postwar period. In the late 1940s and 1950s Commonwealth countries were encouraged to supply labour for the British workplace. Factory hands, transport employees and nurses were targeted and many settled in places where they could identify more readily with their neighbours. In the early 20th century there was an influx of Jewish refugees fleeing persecution and they were concentrated in Didsbury and around Prestwich. In the second half of the century Commonwealth Asian families came to Longsight and Chinese settled in the city centre. Moss Side housed most of the West Indian population and along with the other ethnic minorities helped to provide a greater variety of life and culture into modern Manchester. As well as finding pots and pans for sale from pavement displays, shoppers came across yams, mangoes, sarongs and saris as bhangra, calypso and ska music drifted through the air. The aroma of fish and chips blends well with rogan josh, sweet and sour pork and pan fried chicken.

Above: Woolworth's fronted St Mary's Gate on the corner with Deansgate in 1955 under the shadow of the impressive Royal Exchange building. The old cotton exchange is now home to a variety of gift and specialist shops, fashion outlets, antique dealers and restaurants on its three floors. Also within its walls we can find the theatre in the round that was created at the time when Manchester was reconstructing its city centre. A conglomeration of retail outlets now trade from the Woolworth's site but 50 years ago the original five and ten cent store had this position to itself. Frank Winfield Woolworth brought the first of his American chain stores to Britain in 1909 and by the 1930s it seemed that the company was trading on every town's main shopping street. So successful did they become at infiltrating our lives that we came to regard them as a British institution. The goods were cheap and cheerful and well suited to the pockets of youngsters stuck for a reasonably priced Christmas gift for a member of the family that they could afford from the meagre contents of their piggy banks. A box of bath salts did for granny and mum was bound to appreciate a sweet smelling tin of talc. On Christmas Day he was thanked for his generosity and the 'smellies' were put into the bathroom cabinet alongside the identical ones he had got them for their birthdays... whatever will we do now!!

The January sales were a special occasion when real bargains could be located, or so we thought. They were also an opportunity for stores to generate some business in the lull after Christmas when families usually tightened their belts having spent up buying presents for their children. We still have such sales, but their significance has been eroded by the frequency with which they seem to appear, especially when it comes to the likes of the big furniture chains that always seem to have offers that must end on Sunday. Oldham Street's C & A, now sadly a defunct company, prided itself on offering a mixture of fashion and value and the crowds obviously agreed with that in 1948. Clothing was still rationed, as can be seen from the poster offering certain items at half coupon rate, so items had to be chosen carefully. The number of shoppers wishing to take advantage of the sale had grown to such a crowd that the police were out in force trying to maintain some semblance of order, but they found a queue at a soccer turnstile easier to control than a mob of fashion conscious women. During the war they had suffered the constraints of utility clothing and short hemlines as material was preserved, but now they were ready for the romantic new look designed by Christian Dior. Harold Wilson at the Board of Trade condemned it as frivolous, but women ignored him. What did he know about soft shoulders, handspan waists and full billowing, calf length skirts?

Above: From Pall Mall to Cross Street and the Royal Exchange beyond this section of Market Street was alive with shoppers in 1957. A solitary bobby walked up from the direction of Dolcis, passing the tobacconist who would blend a selection of aromatic pipe tobaccos just to a customer's liking. There were glass topped trays of the finest Virginian, Turkish and Balkan Sobranie varieties as well as speciality brands that included Three Nuns' round swirls of smoking pleasure. The shopkeeper even stocked thick twist for the hardbitten old timer who liked to cut a plug with his penknife before ramming it into the bowl of his pipe with a horned and blackened thumb. The clouds of smoke that engulfed a pipe smoker brought back memories of the Manchester smogs, but the smell was surprisingly pleasant. You could always tell that a man smoked a pipe by the little holes in the front of his shirt where careless sparks had escaped from his briar. As the policeman continued on his beat people smiled and nodded a good morning, which at the time was very reassuring. On the odd occasion we see a member of the law walking the streets now he is usually with a colleague for safety and if a pedestrian smiles at another person on the pavement he is thought to be odd or indulging in some form of harassment.

Top right: In 1961 Marks and Spencer moved across the road to open this new store, seen here some two years after it opened. The bus is heading from St Mary's Gate and onto Market Street. Cross Street and Corporation Street run to the right and left on the other side of the department store. This building was one of many obliterated in the IRA attack on 15 June 1996 when a 3,000 lb car bomb exploded. A pillar box that somehow remained largely undamaged has since been resited on its original spot on the pavement on Corporation Street near to a memorial plaque. A new Marks and Spencer, the world's largest branch of this famous chain store with 32,500 square feet of floor space, has since appeared on the site and is connected to the Arndale Centre by a new bridge. However, half of the building has now been sold to Selfridge's. The man walking towards the camera is crossing Exchange Street which opens out into St Ann's Square. Behind him the woman keenly examining the jewellery in the shop window was possibly checking on the price and style of engagement rings as she might have been returning the following week with her intended. If she had left it 40 years until her return it would not have mattered. Kay's is still there, though the cost might have increased in the meantime.

Below: Conran Street, at the corner with Carisbrook Street, close to its market, is in the heart of Harpurhey. Although added to the borough of Manchester in 1885 at the same time as Bradford and Rusholme, it has enjoyed keeping some of its own identity. Along with neighbouring Collyhurst, Harpurhey has regarded itself as being one of the places from where true Mancunians originate. Even as far away as Langley in Middleton the residents there still regard Manchester as their spiritual home, particularly if their families came from these streets at one time. Some of the famous names in soccer came from north Manchester, men who showed a determination and true grit forged in more humble surroundings. It is no coincidence that Nobby Stiles, Paul Scholes, Tommy Booth and Brian Kidd sweated blood for City or United and none of whom could ever be called a shrinking violet. In 1959 we had come to the end of the grey days of shortages and tightened belts as goods were well within the price range that we could afford. Even items that were once luxuries, such as washing machines and televisions, were becoming standard equipment. We were still basically an honest set of people. Who today would leave a moped unattended outside a shop without padlocking it firmly to a drainpipe?

ON THE MOVE

Traffic jams, crowded carriageways and vehicles grinding to a halt are not a modern phenomenon as can be seen from this 1939 scene. Market Street is now pedestrianised but it was once one of the busiest routes around the city. Great names along here at the time included Boydell Brothers' merchant tailors, the Albion Hotel and Yates Wine Lodge, but the women on the pavement were not interested in the last two of those establishments for they had shopping to do on what must have been a chilly day as they were well wrapped up against the weather. This used to be called Market Stead Lane and was part of the 18th century development of the town that spread eastward here and south along Deansgate.

Many of the cars in the photograph had running boards, reminiscent of those used in gangster movies about the era when Al Capone or Legs Diamond sprayed their enemies with machinegun fire or when escaping from Eliot Ness and his Untouchables. The stern, rectangular lines of these old models are far removed from the sleek, swept back designs that we have now. Older readers may recall having to crank them into life with a starting handle in cold weather. Mum or one of the children pumped the accelerator pedal as dad turned the engine over in an effort to catch the very moment that it spluttered into life so that he could leap back into the driving seat before it died on him.

Above: E Simpson might have been a fine butcher but his grammar was not too good, as evidenced by the placing of the apostrophe in the lettering on the back of the van involved in this accident in 1943. That particular punctuation mark seems to have given people great problems for many a year. Just think of the number of little cafés that advertise 'tea's' or shops that are having 'sale's'. Yet adults today criticise the spelling and grammar of the young when their own parents were just as bad. But the Simpson van had more to worry about than dotting an 'i' or crossing a 't' because its bangers had gone off long before they reached the frying pan.

moving. From the angle of the vehicles it would seem that the lorry driver was at fault, having turned across in front of the van. Accidents at night during the blackout were quite frequent, but there was no such excuse in this case.

Top: The French have a saying that, in effect, means that even as life moves on in essence nothing really changes. That holds true for the city's transport system. In 1930 this tram stop on Oxford Road would have been viewed as a period piece half a century later, but in the 21st century it merely appears to be part of the evolution that has brought us the modern vehicles that criss cross the centre on a daily basis. The shape and lines of the coachwork may have altered but the basic job that they do in the field of public transport is just as it was. Unwary visitors to Manchester may be surprised to see tracks cutting across the roadway once again but Mancunians have become well used to their reappearance as part of the fabric of city life. Nostalgia buffs revelled in seeing the system reintroduced even if most of them were far too young to remember the originals that clanked their way backwards and forwards in a manner immortalised in song by the late Judy Garland's 'Trolley Song' in the 1944 movie 'Meet me in St Louis'. Perhaps some local film maker could produce a sequel, such as 'Meet me in St Peter's Square', though the title lacks a certain je ne sais quoi, to go back to French sayings once more.

The accident on Rochdale Road had occurred at the junction with Queen's Road, a notoriously dangerous crossroads in Collyhurst, just a couple of miles north of the city centre on the A664 heading out past Boggart Hole Clough towards Blackley. The police had turned out in force to lend assistance and keep other traffic

Above: The age of steam locomotives is one that fills most of us old enough to remember the puffing giants with a nostalgia that is fuelled by frequent trips down memory lane organised by railway buffs who have lovingly preserved old lines and rolling stock. Whenever there is an opportunity to see these marvels of engineering crowds gather to turn back the clock and gaze at the footplates wishing that they could step up into the cab and help stoke the boiler or pull on the whistle. Usually they have to be satisfied with short journey in one of the old carriages with the drop down sash windows. Sometimes Thomas the Tank and the Fat Controller are due to make an appearance and it is amazing how caring parents suddenly become. They decide that it would be a good day out for their children to visit Ramsbottom or Embsay and see these old locomotives in action. We know which ones are really the big kids. After all, was it not dad who bought that Hornby set for his two month old son last Christmas? He was trying to relive the day in 1957 when he got on board the excursion train at Victoria, piloted by engine 45642 'Boscawen'. The Victoria line was started by Manchester and Leeds Railway in 1844 and the station enlarged by Lancashire and Yorkshire Railway.

We cannot see what is in this young lad's left hand, but it could have been an exercise book in which he carefully recorded the engine numbers of the locomotives that thundered into Central Station in 1955. Now in his 60s does he still have that dog-eared record of the days he spent on such innocent pursuits tucked away in a tin box in the attic? Is it gathering dust along with other books full of cricket scores when he played imaginary matches for Lancashire as Geoff Edrich or Brian Statham using two small hexagonal metal rollers in a game called 'Howzat'? Up in the rafters there are Dinky cars, lead soldiers and a cap gun that are part of the culture of his childhood. Today, whenever he walks along Windmill Street he must feel a tingle looking up at the Great Northern Railway name that is still spelled out on the warehouse next to G-Mex, as the station became. Central Station was a magnificent piece of architecture that was completed in 1880 and included an impressive 210 foot roof span. There was a covered walkway across the street linking it directly into the Midland Hotel. Closure came in May 1969, by which time this boy's interests had moved onto more adult themes. After some time as a car park it became the exhibition centre and concert hall.

The long line of buses in Portland Street shows how we still relied heavily on public transport in 1955 to get us about because wholesale car ownership was not yet the norm, though the time when it became a necessity rather than a luxury was not too far away. The chap on the bicycle seems to have the right idea because at least he is on the move. This time of day is known as the rush hour, but it is not a description that fits easily with the scene of lines of gridlocked traffic. It would be more appropriate to call it snail hour as stationary exhausts pump out their toxic fumes into the surrounding environment. In the early 1950s these emissions, mixed with the smoke from factory chimneys and domestic coal fires, produced such filthy smogs that brought people with respiratory problems to their knees. A crisply starched shirt that was virgin white in the morning was a grey, black flecked caricature of its former self come night-time. Some of the buses on view had the letter X placed after their route number. This signified that they only operated during peak times and then just on the busiest part of the route.

Left: Rochdale Road in 1959 was unusually quiet. Even back then the scene was often busier than we can see here, though the amount of traffic today far outnumbers what we had in those 'never had it so good' times that Harold Macmillan liked to remind us of as he retained power in October's general election. He did have a point because we were becoming a more affluent society, as illustrated by the rise in private car ownership. With that symbol of good living came the problem of safety on our roads. Despite our scorn of the driving standards of Italians and the French, our own record was none too rosy. Back in the 1930s we had one of the worst set of casualty statistics in the western world, leading us to adopt various measures such as driving tests, pedestrian crossings and cats' eye road studs in an effort to improve matters. In the second half of the last century there were further road safety campaigns, such as the one in evidence here where motorists were reminded by placards to take greater care. In schools cycling proficiency schemes were launched and lessons given to children about the dangers on our roads via Stop, Look and Listen, the Tufty Club and the Green Cross Code. As television became a popular medium adverts were run, often using sporting personalities to reinforce the safety message.

Below: Parking was not too much of a problem near our football grounds in 1960, provided you set off early. At United's ground there was room on the railway lines alongside Trafford Park Road and near Maine Road there were innumerable little side streets where a lad would gladly keep an eye your motor for a few coppers. Not that he really did, but it was a way of ensuring that he had not scratched a rude message on the paintwork whilst you were preoccupied with watching Dave Ewing flatten yet another unwary centre forward. For those of us without cars or had left it to the last minute as we finished off a pre match pint and pie, there were the football specials. These buses on Aytoun Street were soon packed to the gunwales with supporters wearing coloured scarves, rosettes and waving rattles. When the final whistle blew it was a mad scramble back to where the transport was lined up, a quick push and shove and you were ready to be whisked back to the departure point and home in time to listen to what was left of Eamonn Andrews' 'Sports Report' before you read the Football Pink. Of course, all this took place on a Saturday, with the action starting at 3 pm. You knew where your team was in the league by teatime, rather than as happens nowadays to suit its satellite fancy. You cannot imagine Harry Gregg saving a shot from Bill McAdams at 2.15 on a pay per view Sunday afternoon.

Right: The last of the trolley buses left Ashton under Lyne in 1966. We might have been winning the World Cup, but we were losing a form of transport that future generations will probably regard as a quirky piece of 20th century transport history. It was fitting that Ashton under Lyne corporation should send out this vehicle on its final journey as the first services were run along Ashton Old Road. With their arms reaching up to the power lines above they provided a natural link between the old tram system and the era of the petrol engined buses. After World War I it was appreciated that trams were too inflexible in dealing with the rising number of passengers and, as they were restricted by the tracks they followed, added to congestion on the streets as the motor car became more popular. It made sense to use some of the established cabling to power the trolley buses that could move more freely than their predecessors in public transport. For 40 years they were a common sight, though initially taking some getting used to. Pedestrians were accustomed to hearing the clanking of the trams as they approached and the quiet arrival of a trolley bus caught some unawares. Following a spate of accidents some dubbed them 'the silent death'. During World War II they became invaluable as many petrol buses were mothballed, their fuel being needed for the war effort.

Left It was buses like this one that were involved in the evacuation of patients from hospitals that had been damaged in World War II air raid attacks. Equipped with its own stretchers, the vehicles were a useful extension of the ambulance service, and were capable of transporting a greater number of injured people from bomb damaged areas. Parts of the city of Manchester were completely devastated during the war. The enemy made concentrated attacks on the city during the winter of 1940-41, and six hundred people from Manchester and the surrounding area died during the Christmas bombing raids. Whole areas of the city were destroyed. This

Manchester Corporation single-deck bus was introduced to the fleet between 1937-1939 and it is believed to be a streamliner body on a Mancunian chassis.

Left: Five-thirty at the end of another long, hard day, and everybody wants to get home as fast as possible. But no one is going anywhere in a hurry in this traffic jam.... It was 1953 when these crowds of commuters were caught on camera, and in the heyday of public transport chaotic scenes like this were repeated at the end of every working day. Before and during World War II the motor car was viewed as something of a middle class status symbol which was beyond the reach of the ordinary person in the street. Fortunately there were plenty of buses and fares were cheap, and whether you were going to work or to a dance you would more than likely hop on a bus or trolley bus. The two Crossley bodied Manchester Corporation buses in the foreground were both on the No 93 Central Station route. During the 1950s fourteen different major operators ran bus services in Greater Manchester, each fleet having its own individual livery. One-man operation was introduced in 1958.

Above: The year was 1959, and car enthusiasts will recognise the familiar Morris Traveller, the Humber, the Morris (Oxford?) and the classic lines of the homely old Ford Popular among the queue of vehicles entering the car park at Old Trafford Cricket Ground on Great Stone Road. The site was first used as a cricket ground in 1857. They could well be queueing up to watch the test match against India, which was notable as batsman Geoff Pullar became the first Lancashire player to score a test century at Old Trafford. A memorable match had been played at the ground three years earlier in 1956, when Jim Laker, playing for England, got 19 wickets in the Test Match against Australia in July. In the first innings he took ten for fifty-three and in the second he took nine for thirty-seven. His partner Tony Lock took the other wicket. Interestingly, the highest individual score at an Old Trafford Test Match was made by Australian R B Simpson, who scored 311 against England in 1964. In the same match Ken Barrington scored 256 against Australia; Australia made 656 for eight declared.

Below: Somewhere along the line Manchester acquired a rather unfair reputation as being the city where it always rains. On this photograph, however, which dates back to 1934, it is the city of fog and rain. You might be forgiven for thinking that the picture was taken one dismal winter's evening, but this line of traffic halted by the police officer on point duty was caught on camera in the middle of the day. Thousands of coal fires around the city added their smoke to the fog, creating what came to be known as smog - a deadly mixture of smoke and fog that turned day to night. Fog descended on Manchester with monotonous regularity, as it did in all large cities, and the acrid smell and taste of soot hung in the air. Pedestrians resorted to tying scarves across their noses and mouths while vehicles crept along the city's roads at a snail's pace, following the tail lights of the car in front. In 1952 Manchester was one of the first cities to introduce smokeless zones.

Right: This photograph, taken in 1946, reminds us of just how popular Belle Vue once was. The leisure complex was often described as the 'showground of the world'; certainly its exhibition halls were at one time the largest outside London. Many of its facilities were closed down during World War II, and parts of the grounds were requisitioned by the government for military use. Much of it did remain open, however, and the pleasure grounds became a mecca for war weary people in search of diversion. Belle Vue was at the height of its popularity during the post war boom between the mid 1940s and early 1950s, when literally millions converged upon the pleasure grounds. Losses that had been suffered during the war were made up; new animals were acquired for the zoo, the buildings were renovated, and more facilities introduced. There had been a pleasure park on the site since 1836, when entrepreneur John Jennison leased the land for six months to develop his ideas for a pleasure garden that would serve the people of Manchester. It took off in a big way, and Jennison established a deer paddock, gardens, boating lakes, a maze, and archery and cricket facilities.

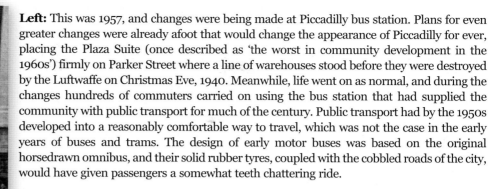

Left: This was 1957, and changes were being made at Piccadilly bus station. Plans for even greater changes were already afoot that would change the appearance of Piccadilly for ever, placing the Plaza Suite (once described as 'the worst in community development in the 1960s') firmly on Parker Street where a line of warehouses stood before they were destroyed by the Luftwaffe on Christmas Eve, 1940. Meanwhile, life went on as normal, and during the changes hundreds of commuters carried on using the bus station that had supplied the community with public transport for much of the century. Public transport had by the 1950s developed into a reasonably comfortable way to travel, which was not the case in the early years of buses and trams. The design of early motor buses was based on the original horsedrawn omnibus, and their solid rubber tyres, coupled with the cobbled roads of the city, would have given passengers a somewhat teeth chattering ride.

Below: Piccadilly in 1957 was vastly different from the central square with its smart shops and the Plaza Suite that we are familiar with today. But if we go back even further to the pre-war years, Piccadilly was different again, and older Mancunians will remember the warehouses of Staines Inlaid Linoleum, Peel, Watson & Co and J Templeton & Co that bordered Parker Street and Portland Street until the Luftwaffe reduced them to a heap of smoking rubble on the evening of Christmas Eve 1940. That raid was a particularly bad one. Searchlights raked the sky seeking the elusive German planes. The flares they dropped lit up the city as wave after wave of German bombers passed overhead, dropping their deadly load of high explosive bombs across Manchester. The Parker Street warehouses were hit badly, and fed by fractured gas mains the whole row was soon a blazing inferno. Exhausted ARP wardens and firemen worked bravely on though incendiary bombs were falling around them. The blaze raged on for many hours, and eventually it was realised that the only way to fight the fires effectually was to blow up the untouched buildings that lay in the path of the fire.

MAKING A LIVING

Above: A woman's place is by the kitchen sink, doing the housework and bringing up the children. Try and tell that to Louise Lyans as she received instruction from Jim Botterill in the art of driving a tram. She was Manchester's first woman tram driver, but was not really a trail blazer. Elsewhere women were driving ambulances, buses and jeeps in both military and civilian roles. The trend had begun in the 1914-18 War when women rolled up their sleeves and took over traditional positions on the factory floor and behind the wheel. Government had not given them the vote, but they rallied behind the flag in the service of the nation. It was even more apparent in World War II as munitions works, transport and agriculture all owed women a huge vote of thanks. The tram Louise was driving was the latest development from the one horse bus service from Pendleton to Market Street that first ran in 1824. Horse drawn trams operated from 1877 until 1903, being superseded by electric trams that continued to serve the city for nearly 50 years. When the first phase of the new supertrams was finished in 1991, linking Bury and Altrincham via Manchester, Louise might have been forgiven for regarding them as old hat. She had seen it all before from inside the cab.

It is remarkable that we managed to survive and even enjoy our lives before we had political correctness, equal opportunities and dictates against every -ism under the sun. Added to these is the health and safety lobby, possibly one of the nation's biggest growth industries of the last 20 years. The mind boggles at what it would have made of these workers at Manchester Abattoir in 1950. There is blood from the carcasses dripping all over the floor and stains on the men's so-called white coats. The flat hat never left the head of one member of this trio and rumour had it that he kept it on in the bath. Imagine his attitude if he had to don a hairnet and put on a pretty white hat when he came to work. How times have changed, because even the humble butcher's shop no longer has rabbits and poultry hanging on hooks as they acquire an appropriately gamey smell. You cannot have a piece of corned beef stored within half a mile of a nice juicy sirloin and hands need washing so often that they end up looking as though they belong to Mrs Mopp. What was so wrong with wiping them on your overalls or picking up a chop dropped on the floor and giving it a quick rinse under the tap? A bit of sawdust put hairs on your chest.

same company after it had been absorbed into Hawker Siddeley Aviation or, in 1977 when nationalisation took it into British Aerospace. Whatever the title, this large family of employees were proud to work for a company which ranks high in the world of aeroplane builders. The company itself was formed in Manchester on New Year's Day 1910 by Alliott Verdon Roe and his brother Humphrey. It was A V Roe who claimed the distinction of being the first Englishman to fly in a powered aeroplane of his own design just two years earlier. The company trade name of AVRO soon became recognised as one of the leaders in the fledgling aviation industry.

Below: The Type E being transported to London Road (now Piccadilly) Station for the train journey down to Brooklands in Surrey for test flying. Brooklands, of course, was the Mecca of the flying pioneers at the time.

Right: In July 1912 Avro flew one of its Type 500s to Old Trafford, Manchester to allow the company's employees to see one of their aeroplanes in flight for the first time. The aircraft is shown in a field outside the works of Robert Carlyle Ltd.

Above: An Avro E aeroplane under construction at the company's first manufacturing facility at Brownsfield Mill in 1912. After completion the aircraft had to be dismantled for transportation to the flying field. In Manchester there must be few people who have not had relatives or friends working at some time for Avro, the aircraft manufacturers. In succeeding generations they would have worked for the

Below: In 1833 an English candle maker, William Procter, and an Irish soap maker, James Gamble, married two sisters. Four years later, they formed a partnership which was to become the Procter and Gamble Company. The company grew quickly and, in the late 1920s, contemplated its first move outside North America. Europe was still getting over the ravages of the Great War and many businesses were going through hard times. Thomas Hedley, a soap making company based in Newcastle, was such an organisation. Procter and Gamble took them over in 1930. Many American brands were quickly introduced into the British market. The new parent company's dynamic approach soon saw the Newcastle factory at full stretch so that a new site was needed. Trafford Park in Manchester proved to be ideal. The Trafford Park estates had been on the grounds of Sir Humphrey de Trafford's mansion. He disliked seeing merchant ships sailing past his property on

the newly-constructed Ship Canal and sold the estate! Eventually the park was sold as lots to any company that wanted to buy. In 1931 ten acres were leased to Procter and Gamble at 9d a square yard and the land was purchased outright in 1933. The original factory took three years to build. It was the largest soap and candle factory in the world and it was officially opened in 1934.

Top right: The Auxiliary Fire Service did a lot of sterling work alongside the regular Fire Department during World War II, and the green engines of the AFS could often be observed at the scene of an air raid. High explosive bombing would destroy property, fracturing gas mains and creating huge fire storms that were fed by the often flammable contents of warehouses and shops. This 1939 photograph shows an inspection of the AFS and their appliances. When a fire was reported, often by one of the

fire watchers who were recruited from those men who were either too old to fight or were in a reserved occupation, the petrol operated pumps seen here would be towed to the scene of the blaze and would pump water from a nearby dam or a supply of static water. During the war the basements of bombed out buildings were often deliberately flooded to provide a static water supply for the use of fire fighters.

Bottom right: Traditionally, British men have been regarded as the bread winners, going out to work every day to keep their wives and families. Their women folk saw to the children, shopped

for food every day, made the meals, cleaned the house, and washed and ironed the family's clothes. The Second World War changed the way of life for hundreds of men and women, turning generations of tradition upside down. When Britain's men were called into military service, women found themselves doing jobs they had never done before. Many of them worked in machine shops and engineering factories, turning out armaments and aeroplane parts, work that had always been looked on as 'jobs for the men'. Women did a good job - and what is more, they found themselves enjoying the work. After the war many of them didn't want to give up their jobs and go back to their old lives. They had become used to the degree of independence that a weekly wage gave them. Suddenly they could afford to buy clothes and makeup and treats for the children.

These women captured by the camera worked in a Manchester ordnance factory, and are seen here turning the shell caps.

Right: Even when middle aged a street trader was still referred to as a barrow boy. It was a hard life trying to make ends meet by attempting to attract custom to his humble point of sale in Market Place. He used a mixture of wit and vocal power to tempt shoppers his way, but, for the moment, seems to be taking a little rest in this 1958 photograph. That he dressed in a suit was not unusual because most men went into the city in those days much more formally dressed than ever they do now. It was not quite a pinstripe, but it was a jacket and trousers and he would have been horrified to come across a bank manager wearing what establishments refer to as business casual. To him it would have meant just plain scruffy. Behind him the new building work was only a foretaste of the changes to come on Market Place, that part of medieval Manchester that had been the scene of rioting against high bread prices in 1795. The cavalry quelled that disturbance, just as it did more dreadfully in the 1819 Peterloo massacre.

Left: After the first world war the government promised servicemen returning from their duties overseas that they would be coming back to a land fit for heroes. They were empty promises as the country nosedived into the years of economic depression that brought us a slump, strikes and hardship. Similar promises were made in 1945 and this time there was some truth in the assurances that were given, though it was hardly Utopia in the early postwar period. The electorate turned to Clement Attlee's Labour party to pave the way and the National Health Service came into being and immediate work began on restoring the nation's housing stocks. The prewar slums had become even worse in the intervening years and so many houses had been demolished in air raids that replacements were a matter of some urgency. At least Manchester could hold its head up high as it was one of the most farsighted of boroughs in the inter war years, building over 27,000 new council houses. Helped in part by American financial aid under the Marshall Plan, new homes rose from the ashes. Wythenshawe, part of the borough since 1931, was intended to be a largely self sufficient garden city, though it never quite achieved that aim in full. Here, in 1950, work was in progress building shops and maisonettes on Greenbrow Road, Newall Green. Many former urban dwellers got to enjoy front and back gardens for the first time.

Above: Hour upon hour of joy could be gained from browsing through the books piled high in Sherratt and Hughes on Cross Street. It was a comfortable place in which to spend an afternoon immersed in the language of the classic writers and those breaking into the world of popular literature. Georgette Heyer happily rubbed shoulders with Charles Dickens and there was an endless supply of Enid Blyton fare for the younger reader. Some visitors never bought a book but popped in from the office each lunchtime, read a chapter of a novel and returned on subsequent days until they had finished the whole book. Colonel John Hunt's 'Our Everest Adventure' was one of the bestsellers in 1954, recounting the conquering of the world's highest peak by the expedition he had led to the Himalayas the previous year. Sherratt and Hughes was also the bookshop where GCE 'O' and 'A' level students could buy their Latin primers, geometry books and log tables. It had a homely feel that only individual and independent shops can offer.

Left: At first sight this appears to belong to a section on the wartime blitz, but the date is wrong as we are now in 1957. This fire at Paulden's department store on Stretford Road, next to Cavendish Street, destroyed a building that had stood on this spot since 1879. What a dramatic end it came to and what can better illustrate the courage of the firefighting crew than the sight of them striving to quell the flames as tons of masonry come crashing down around their ears. Their headquarters were on London Road, opposite the railway station, in that attractive baroque style building that was designed and built by Woodhouse, Willoughby and Langham from 1904-1906. Its architectural merit was recognised by being given Grade II listed status. The central courtyard includes a training tower and a series of balconies in whose tenements 40 firemen once lived. The first fire brigades were run by insurance companies, anxious to keep a check on the high incidence of fire in our crowded towns in the early 19th century. The close proximity of properties to each other and the lack of common sense in taking safety precautions forced the insurers' hands as they were paying out with too much frequency for their liking. Eventually, local councils gradually assumed control and Manchester's own fire station was established in Town Yard where the town hall now stands.

Below: There was a time when most women were able to make their own clothes, run up a set of curtains and make a set of cushion covers. In 1959 this pair was on Barlow Moor Road, Chorlton-cum-Hardy demonstrating the latest in the line of Singer models that was on the market. The woman on the left wore her dress at the fashionable mid calf length with a wide sweeping skirt over a petticoat that swung attractively whenever she did a twirl. By the end of the following decade skirts would be more like pelmets and the length of time it took to make a mini or micro shortened in direct proportion. Back home girls were taught to use knitting needles and interpret patterns and instructions such as 'psso' as they passed each slip stitch over. Socks were darned and elbow patches attached to dad's best jacket. If the slightest tear appeared in a piece of material it was out with the needle and thread or a quick treadle on the sewing machine to put it right. We now live in a throwaway society that has adopted the attitude of when it is worn then discard it. Our parents thought differently for they lived a life of make and mend. Mum could carry on a conversation, watch 'Emergency Ward 10' on the television and knit a pair of bootees for next door's new arrival all at the same time.

BIRD'S EYE VIEW

This scene was captured looking along Deansgate, to the right, as it leads to Victoria Street where the cathedral and Chetham's School are situated. In the centre the Irwell heads the same way before almost joining them at Exchange Station. Dr Beeching had not reared his ugly head in 1959 and the days of his cuts were still a few years away. On the face of it most of his reforms were aimed at rural lines and stations, but they had their knock on effect in the city as services were rescheduled. Going back in time to 1830 when the first passenger service was established, it seems strange that it should be between Manchester and Liverpool, linking those two arch rivals in everything from commerce to pop music. Of course, by 1841 there were more than 1,300 miles of track in Britain and the nature of our lives changed as the population became so much more mobile as it found it easier to move around the country in search of employment. In 1849 Exchange Station became the fourth to open in Manchester, though it was as much an add-on to Victoria Station as anything else. Victoria had opened on Hunt's Bank in 1844 and when the Exchange, named for the nearby Cotton Exchange, was built the continued platform with Victoria measured 2,194 feet, the longest in Britain. Exchange Station was demolished in 1969 and became a car park.

Barton Power Station was pumping out its fumes in 1958 on the Davyhulme side of the Manchester Ship Canal, across the way from Eccles and its famous currant cakes. The Victorian age was a time when rail travel and haulage expanded rapidly, so it was odd to see a new canal being built in 1887. There was good reason, for Manchester had come to depend upon Liverpool's powerful position. Allied with the port charges were high rail tariffs for moving freight and it was apparent good sense to try to counter the cost by seeking alternatives. Manchester was able to develop its own niche as a port and do away with the rail costs by opening the Ship Canal in 1894. The new artery also helped boost engineering in Trafford Park. It was a marvel of Victorian technology as the canal included an aqueduct across its width that carried the Bridgewater Canal. Barton Road swing bridge was another example of fine engineering, though lengthy traffic jams built up here in the days before the motorway bridge was built in the mid 1960s. Until about then rowing boats were still being sculled across the canal at the penny ferry in Irlam. The swing bridge was very useful to pupils at Salford's De La Salle Grammar School as it provided them with a good excuse for being late in a morning, though headmaster Brother Columba had heard it all before. Old Barton Road, the little lane meandering towards the top of the photograph, is heading almost towards the Trafford Centre shopping complex.

Enfolded in the embrace of the Town Hall extension, the perfectly circular Manchester Central Library building provides us with an immediate point of reference, while nearby Albert Square provides and open space in the city centre in front of the Town Hall. The library, completed in 1934, was at that time the largest public library in the country. Two competitions had been held for a design for the library building and the Town Hall extension. Vincent Harris presented a design for both buildings - and both were chosen. The site for the library, which was chosen partly for its proximity to the city centre, was cleared in 1929, and Prime Minister Ramsay McDonald laid the foundation stone on 6th May 1930. King George V declared the library officially open at a ceremony held on 17th July 1934. The building's elegant rotunda houses the reference section and an impressive entry from St Peter's Square boasts a two storey portico with six elegant columns. The library's collection of works is an impressive one, and in pride of place is a collection of around 30 ancient books which were printed before 1501.

Left: The new city centre is beginning to emerge, as can be seen here in the bottom right corner where the Plaza complex of buildings can just be made out. The Piccadilly redevelopment was the tip of the iceberg; much of the central area around Market Street and Corporation Street was demolished in the 1960s. The Arndale Centre and other modern buildings replaced the old city streets. At the top of the photograph the Cooperative Insurance Society building rises from the surrounding buildings like a gigantic accusing finger. To the left of the CIS building Cheetham Hill and Corporation Street sweep past Victoria Station, another familiar landmark.

Travellers hurrying for a train rarely have the time to stop and admire their surroundings, but those who do will surely be thankful that the restaurant escaped the redeveloper's drawing board. The Victorians took a lot of trouble to make buildings pleasing to the eye; the ornate 'Refreshment Room ' signs are typical of the times.

Below: The 36 mile long Manchester Ship Canal heads in the direction of Old Trafford before making a dramatic sweep to the left, past Pomona Docks and out towards Ordsall. Timber was for many years a major import to the bustling Salford Docks. Vessels headed up the Canal bringing china clay from Cornwall, Egyptian cotton from Alexandria and Middle East produce from ports in the Mediterranean. When war broke out in 1939, the Manchester Liners fleet had a total of 10 vessels. The merchant ships were repainted in camouflage livery, and carried no names or markings. Three of them were lost during the war; the third vessel, 'Manchester City' was requisitioned by the Admiralty. Among the many ships torpedoed at sea, 'Manchester City' managed to survive and remained in service until 1964. Air raids during 1940-41 targeted the docks and the many factories in the surrounding area, but the Company succeeded in keeping the waterway open. Peace eventually returned; operations at the docks got back to normal and vessels resumed their smart pre war livery, slowly reverting to their peace time activities. The canal was very busy during the 1950s. Between 1954 and 1974 the annua

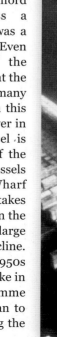

Above: A dramatic photograph of Salford Docks, giving us a closer view of the rows of vast warehouses that line the dockside, and the number of large vessels discharging cargo in No 9 Dock. A large ship is docked at Trafford Wharf in the foreground.

The Manchester Ship Canal was built towards the end of the 19th Century as an answer to high railway charges and rocketing charges at Liverpool Docks. The building started in November 1887, and Queen Victoria herself declared the Manchester Ship Canal open in May, 1894. Immediately trade took off, justifying the £15 million it cost to build. 925,000 tons of traffic entered the Port of Manchester in its first year. Less than a hundred years later the heyday of the Manchester Ship Canal was over, and grain elevators were demolished and rail tracks torn up. In the 1990s, however, a new lease of life was given to Salford Docks with the Salford Quay Development. The old docks were divided into water parks, a marina was built and No 7 Dock was stocked with fish for anglers. With an eye to the leisure industry, hotels and leisure facilities were built and new office blocks and houses were constructed.

Right: This view of Salford Docks, captured in March 1972, gives us some idea of the immensity of what things must have been like in the heyday of the Manchester Ship Canal. The docks, though largely in Salford and Stretford, were nevertheless a Manchester enterprise and the port was a thriving centre for Britain's exports. Even the high viewpoint cannot dwarf the enormous gantries at Number 2 Dock at the bottom left of the photograph. How many men spent their entire working life in this truly amazing environment, like Gulliver in the land of Lilliput? A solitary vessel is docked at No 8 Pier in the centre of the picture, and opposite, a number of vessels along Trafford Wharf. Trafford Wharf Road, the straight road on the right, takes traffic away towards the swing bridge in the distance. By the 1970s the number of large ships using the docks had begun to decline. Strikes staged by dock workers in the 1950s hit the Company hard and a 47 day strike in 1966 severely disrupted programme development. By 1970 customers began to take their cargoes elsewhere; signalling the beginning of the end.

This particular view of Manchester will never be seen again except in the memories of Mancunians. Many will remember the city as it was, before the 1960s development and the building of the Arndale Centre wiped away vast areas of the old and familiar city centre. The trapezoidal building in the right hand corner of the picture is the Rylands Building (now Debenhams and Woolworths), while the CIS Building, not far removed from Victoria Station, can be seen on the top right. The Corn and Produce Exchange, now a complex of shops, forms an elegant triangle alongside Manchester Cathedral in the top centre just below the playground of Chethams School. The school was founded by Humphry Chetham in 1651 to provide a good education for 40 poor boys. Today the school is Chetham's School of Music, internationally famous for the excellence of its musical education and the talent of its students.

Manchester city centre as it was a couple of decades ago, spread out below like a three dimensional map. Slightly off centre towards the top of the photograph we can pick out the walkways and flower beds of Piccadilly Gardens, the bus station and the Plaza Suite site. The Town Hall and its extension and the dramatic Public Library dominate the scene; the YMCA is the almost triangular building next to the library. In Albert Square the Prince Consort's memorial can be seen, taking pride of place in the open square in front of the civic buildings. Statues of other respected Victorian reformers and politicians Bishop James Fraser, John Bright, W E Gladstone and Oliver Heywood remind passing Mancunians of their heritage.

Thomas Worthington designed the tall Gothic canopy that shelters Prince Albert's statue, developing his design from a sketch he had made of a chapel during a visit to Pisa nearly 20 years earlier.

ACKNOWLEDGMENTS

The publishers would like to sincerely thank the following individuals and organisations for their help and contribution to this publication

Manchester Central Library - Archive and Local Studies Unit

Paula Moorhouse

Chris Makepeace

Manchester City FC

Manchester United FC

Len Myatt